Learning About Print in Preschool

Working With Letters, Words, and Beginning Links
With Phonemic Awareness

2ND EDITION

DOROTHY S. STRICKLAND
JUDITH A. SCHICKEDANZ

Part of the Preschool Literacy Collection edited by
Lesley Mandel Morrow

INTERNATIONAL
Reading Association
800 BARKSDALE ROAD, PO BOX 8139
NEWARK, DE 19714-8139, USA
www.reading.org

D1318595

IRA BOARD OF DIRECTORS

The International Reading Association attempts, through its publications, to provide a forum for a wide spectrum of opinions on reading. This policy permits divergent viewpoints without implying the endorsement of the Association.

Executive Editor, Books   Corinne M. Mooney
Developmental Editor   Charlene M. Nichols
Developmental Editor   Tori Mello Bachman
Developmental Editor   Stacey L. Reid
Editorial Production Manager   Shannon T. Fortner
Design and Composition Manager   Anette Schuetz
Project Editor   Stacey L. Reid

Cover   Design, Monotype; Photograph, ©2009 Jupiterimages Corporation and Gwynnith Strickland

Library of Congress Cataloging-in-Publication Data
Strickland, Dorothy S.
    Learning about print in preschool : working with letters, words, and beginning links with phonemic awareness / Dorothy S. Strickland, Judith A. Schickedanz. — 2nd ed.
        p. cm. — (Preschool literacy collection)
    Includes bibliographical references and index.
    ISBN 978-0-87207-477-4
1. Reading (Preschool)   2. Language arts (Preschool)   3. Reading—Phonetic method.   I. Schickedanz, Judith A., 1944–   II. Title.
    LB1140.5.R4S77 2009
    372.46'5--dc22   2008053292

CONTENTS

 Dorothy S. Strickland is the Samuel DeWitt Proctor Professor of Education at Rutgers, the State University of New Jersey in New Brunswick, New Jersey, USA. She received her master's and doctorate degrees from New York University. A former classroom teacher, reading consultant, and learning disabilities specialist, she is a past-president of both the International Reading Association (IRA) and the Reading Hall of Fame.

Strickland received IRA's Outstanding Teacher Educator of Reading Award. She was also the recipient of the Outstanding Educator in the Language Arts Award from the National Council of Teachers of English and the National-Louis University Ferguson Award for Outstanding Contributions to Early Childhood Education. She was a member of the panels that produced *Becoming a Nation of Readers*, *Preventing Reading Difficulties in Young Children*, *Reading for Understanding* (the RAND Reading Study Group report), and the National Early Literacy Panel. Her latest publications include *Literacy Leadership in Early Childhood*, *The Administration and Supervision of Reading Programs* (fourth edition), and *Improving Reading Achievement Through Professional Development.*

A frequent speaker at conferences and professional workshops, Strickland is a strong proponent of ongoing professional development for educators at all levels of instruction.

Judith A. Schickedanz is a Professor in the Department of Literacy and Language, Counseling and Development, in Boston University's School of Education in Boston, Massachusetts, USA. She has taught preschool, worked with many preschool programs throughout her professional career, and started and served for 20 years as the director of the laboratory preschool at Boston University. She also worked in the Boston University Chelsea Public Schools Collaborative, helping to create preschool programs within the school system. Schickedanz has taught courses in child development, early childhood education, and early literacy.

Schickedanz is the author of several books on early reading and writing, including *Much More Than the ABC's* and *Adam's Righting Revolutions*. She was also senior author for four editions of a major child development text: *Understanding Children and Adolescents*. Her most recent book is *Increasing the Power of Instruction: Integration of Language, Literacy, and Math Across the Preschool Day* (2008). A recent book chapter in *Achieving Excellence in Preschool Literacy Instruction* by Justice and Vukelich (2008) focuses on "Increasing Children's Learning by Getting to the Bottom of Their Confusion," and she coauthored a chapter on early literacy in the fourth volume of the *Handbook of Reading Research*, edited by Pearson and Kamil (forthcoming).

Schickedanz has served on several IRA early literacy committees and also served on a National Association for the Education of Young Children committee that updated its accreditation standards. Currently, she is a member of the editorial board of the *International Journal of Early Childhood Education*, published by the Early Childhood Association of Korea, and is a coeditor of the *Asia-Pacific Journal of Research in Early Childhood Education*.

Schickedanz also serves as a literacy foundations and curriculum consultant to several Early Reading First projects and to public preschool and Head Start programs, and she teaches the service learning course at Boston University for the Jumpstart program, a nationwide service program for undergraduate student volunteers with a focus on supporting preschool children's language and literacy development.

GLOSSARY

This glossary provides definitions for many of the specialized literacy terms in this book. These terms are highlighted in boldface type on first occurrence.

alphabet knowledge: The ability to name and write the 26 alphabet letters.

concept of letter: The understanding that letters have distinct shapes, have names, and form words.

concept of word: The understanding that words are composed of letters and separated by spaces.

concepts of print: Children's understandings about the functions (e.g., practical uses), structure (e.g., printed words are separated by spaces), and conventions (e.g., left-to-right, top-to-bottom sequence) of written language.

differentiated instruction: The provision of varied learning situations, as whole-class, small-group, or individual instruction, to meet the needs of students at different levels of reading competence.

invented spelling: An attempt to spell a word whose spelling is not already known, based on knowledge of the spelling system and how it works.

letter strings: Groups of letters written by a child with no attention to sound–letter correspondence.

phonemic awareness: The awareness of the sounds (phonemes) that make up spoken words.

phonics: A way of teaching reading that stresses symbol–sound relationships.

phonological awareness: Awareness of the constituent sounds of words in learning to read and spell.

scaffolding: The process whereby a child's learning occurs in the context of full performance as adults gradually relinquish support.

shared reading: A classroom strategy in which a teacher reads a Big Book with enlarged print and encourages the children to read along on parts that they can remember or predict. Shared reading models the reading process and draws children's attention to print concepts and letter knowledge.

shared writing: A classroom strategy in which the teacher writes down children's own stories about their everyday experiences. These highly contextualized stories are easy for children to read.

skill: An acquired ability to perform well; proficiency.

strategy: A systematic plan for solving a problem.

zone of proximal development (ZPD): The level at which a child finds a task too difficult to complete alone but achievable with the assistance of an adult or more experienced peer.

INTRODUCTION

Interest in early education as a major influence on school readiness has steadily increased in recent years. Educators and policymakers agree that a strong foundation in early literacy is critical. Standards for early literacy are increasing for both children and teachers. In its synthesis of early literacy research, the National Early Literacy Panel (Strickland, 2004; Strickland & Shanahan, 2004) found young children's concepts of print to be a key predictor of later reading outcomes. This book focuses on what preschool teachers and directors of early education programs should know about developing children's print-related knowledge. It offers a variety of instructional strategies that are age- and developmentally appropriate and that include suggestions for making adjustments for the specific needs of individuals. Geared to those ages 3 to 5, the strategies may be simplified for the youngest children in this age range or enriched to provide focused instructional opportunities for older, more advanced children. The book is written in a straightforward style intended to be accessible for any educator faced with increasing demands to foster a wide range of literacy related dispositions and competencies in children.

We learned from literacy coaches and teachers that the first edition of *Learning About Print in Preschool* was a good resource for professional development. They found the book to be accessible to teachers with a wide range of educational backgrounds and experience. Nevertheless, they suggested that they would welcome specific guidelines for its use as a core resource for a long-term inservice effort. Therefore, specific suggestions are provided at the end of each chapter. We hope that by stimulating a professional development program characterized by inquiry, reflection, and action, this book will promote improved literacy learning and teaching.

What Young Children Need to Know About Print

Certain areas of development have direct links to children's success in early reading and school readiness. Oral language, **concepts of print**, **phonological awareness**, and **alphabet knowledge** have strong scientifically based research support as predictors of early literacy success (National Early Literacy Panel Report, 2009; Snow, Burns, & Griffin, 1998). In the first two chapters of this book, we examine what children need to know about concepts of print, alphabet knowledge, and **phonemic awareness** (one aspect of phonological awareness). Chapter 1 defines each area under discussion and offers lists of literacy standards typically found in local and state curriculum guidelines. This chapter places the standards in a learning context by discussing the basic child development principles that support children's learning and that must be in place for children's literacy development to flourish. This is followed in Chapter 2 by a focused discussion of the environmental and adult support required to promote the development of the three critical areas of learning about print: concepts of print, phonemic awareness, and alphabet knowledge.

> Oral language, concepts of print, phonological awareness, and alphabet knowledge have strong scientifically based research support as predictors of early literacy success.

Concepts of Print

Concepts of print refers to children's knowledge of the functions of print and how print works. This includes an understanding that books are read from front to back; an awareness of how print is placed on a page; and an understanding that print carries meaning, has a variety of uses or functions in our lives, and is speech written down. In order to make sense of print, one also needs to understand directionality and comprehend both the **concept of word** (words are composed of letters and separated by spaces) and the **concept of letter** (letters have distinct shapes, have names, and form words). Teachers help children learn these concepts through repeated exposure to and guided activities with books, charts, Big Books, and various types of

Table 1
Typical Standards and Learning Experiences: Concepts of Print

Standards	Learning Experiences
• Understands that print is used for different functions • Understands that speech can be written down • Understands that print carries a message • Understands that illustrations carry meaning but cannot be read • Understands that books have titles and authors • Understands concepts of word—letters are grouped to form words, and words are separated by spaces • Understands concept of directionality—front to back, left to right, and top to bottom movement on a page • Understands that letters function differently than numbers	• Observes varied uses of print for various purposes (e.g., shopping lists, recipes and other simple directions, and letters and messages) and participates in their use • Observes adults writing as they say the words aloud (write aloud) • Participates in composing process by offering ideas and language for others to write down • Attends to print during Big Book activities • Refers to books by their titles; is beginning to understand that a book represents a person's ideas and that this person is the author • Engages in opportunities to draw and "write" independently • Observes and follows along as adults track print from left to right while reading aloud; browses through books from front to back • Participates in opportunities to write own name

functional print. Table 1 shows typical standards and learning experiences for supporting preschool children's development of print concepts.

Phonemic Awareness

Phonemic awareness is the ability to hear, identify, and manipulate the individual sounds (phonemes) in spoken words. It is one level of phonological awareness, the general understanding that words consist of sounds. Phonemic awareness requires more specific **skills** than other levels of phonological awareness; these skills link more directly to **phonics**, which relates sounds to the letters that represent them. Instruction in phonemic awareness may, at times, involve the use of print. That is, it may include linking a letter or letters to sounds in spoken words as they are stressed or isolated by an adult.

Children demonstrate their knowledge of the beginning levels of phonological awareness when they

- Identify and make oral rhymes (e.g., *I can bake a chocolate [cake]. The cat wore a [hat].*)
- Identify and work with syllables in spoken words (e.g., *Jess [one clap], Becky [two claps].*)

Children demonstrate their knowledge of finer aspects of phonological awareness (phonemic awareness) when they

- Identify and work with onsets and rimes in one-syllable words (e.g., The first part of *dog* is /d/. The last part of *cat* is /-at/.)
- Recognize when several words begin with the same sound (e.g., *Wee Willie went walking. Peter Piper picked a peck of pickled peppers.*)
- Identify words that begin with a specific sound (e.g., match and sort pictures according to initial sound)

Phonemic awareness activities are most effective when children are taught to manipulate phonemes and to anchor or code these phonemes with letters. This is sometimes referred to as "phonological awareness with a phonics connection" (Armbruster, Lehr, & Osborn, 2003; National Head Start Summer Teacher Education Program [STEP] Teacher's Manual, 2002). Table 2 shows typical standards and learning experiences for supporting preschool children's development of phonemic awareness.

Table 2
Typical Standards and Learning Experiences: Phonemic Awareness

Standards	Learning Experiences
• Builds on understandings associated with phonological awareness, such as ability to recognize and produce words starting with the same sound • Has the general understanding that letters represent the sounds that make up spoken words (alphabetic principle) • Begins to make some sound–letter associations	• Observes others as they segment spoken words into their individual sounds and use letters to write the sounds • Selects letters to represent individual sounds that a teacher has segmented in a spoken word • Selects a letter to represent an individual sound (usually at the beginning of a word) that he or she has segmented in a spoken word

Alphabet Knowledge

Letter name knowledge, or alphabet knowledge, is an excellent predictor of success in early reading. The fluency (accuracy and speed) with which children recognize letters gives them an advantage in learning to read. Letter names are part of the language used to talk about reading and writing. Alphabet knowledge often indicates children's interest in learning how letters and sounds relate to one another and helps them remember how words are spelled. Some researchers suggest that alphabet knowledge is a byproduct of extensive early literacy experiences. Therefore, simply training children to memorize letters without providing learning in a larger literacy context has proven unsuccessful as a predictor of beginning reading success (Anderson, Hiebert, Scott, & Wilkinson, 1985).

According to Burns, Griffin, and Snow (1999),

> By the end of kindergarten, children should be able to name most of the letters of the alphabet, no matter what order they come in, no matter if they are uppercase or lowercase. And they should do it quickly and effortlessly. (p. 80)

At the preschool level, children are generally expected to know *at least* 10 uppercase letters. Often these are the letters in their own names. Parents and teachers should provide opportunities for children to learn letter names as part of a variety of rich literacy and oral language experiences. Table 3 shows typical standards and learning experiences for supporting preschool children's development of alphabet knowledge.

Table 3
Typical Standards and Learning Experiences: Alphabet Knowledge

Standards	Learning Experiences
• Notices and is able to name letters that begin common logos and names of friends and family members • Understands that letters of the alphabet are special visual graphics that have unique names • Identifies at least 10 letters of the alphabet • Identifies letters in his or her name	• Uses magnetic letters or tiles for play and exploration; plays with alphabet puzzles • Has experiences with alphabet books • Discusses letter names in the context of daily meaningful activities • Observes and participates in experiences where letter names are linked to writing names and other meaningful words

Connecting Child Development With Learning About Print

Although this book focuses on children's knowledge and use of print, the ideas presented here are meant to fit into a much larger picture. Oral language development, storybook reading, comprehension, and writing are all essential elements of early literacy development. It is helpful for us as teachers to examine each of these topics independently and in depth. In practice, we need to apply what we learn about each area in an integrated way because each facet of language and literacy relates to and depends on the others. It is also important for us to put language and literacy in context by considering what is known about children's overall development.

Teachers are often concerned about being planful in the literacy experiences they offer their preschool students, yet they also want literacy to remain engaging for them. They wonder, Am I pushing the children too fast? Will I do harm? How can I balance learning with enjoyment? Teachers who have a solid understanding of child development are better able to incorporate sound literacy instruction into the curriculum in ways that are pleasurable, effective, and age appropriate. The following summary of the multiple pathways of child development includes implications for supporting children's overall readiness to learn. This overview provides a backdrop for the exploration of literacy development—and, more specifically, knowledge about print—that appears in the remaining chapters.

> Teachers who have a solid understanding of child development are better able to incorporate sound literacy instruction into the curriculum in ways that are pleasurable, effective, and age appropriate.

The Multiple Domains of Child Development and Their Implications for Literacy

All the domains of development—physical, social, emotional, cognitive, and language—are essential to a child's personal and academic growth. Families and early childhood educators share concern and responsibility for fostering children's development in each domain.

Physical Development

A major function of early childhood is physical growth and development. At no other time in life is there such a rapid rate of change in size, weight, and body proportions (Allen & Marotz, 1994). Researchers generally refer to children's physical development in terms of

- Gross motor development (control of the large muscles needed for movements such as running, jumping, and climbing)
- Fine motor development (the use of small muscles of the fingers and hands necessary for such tasks as picking up objects, writing, drawing, and managing buttons)
- Sensory–perceptual development (the ability to receive information that comes through the senses and to recognize and interpret it)

Implications for Literacy.　In order to learn, children must be physically healthy. Effective teachers call attention to indications of vision and hearing problems that may influence a child's ability to learn.

Young children also are highly active and are unable to sit still for long periods of time. Effective teachers plan a variety of activities that involve physical movement and active participation. In Figure 1, students are using their large muscles to write with paint outdoors.

Figure 1
Children Write With Paint Outdoors

Social and Emotional Development

By age 3 or 4, most children are part of a peer group (Moore, 1982). Whether in play groups or in school settings, children are expected to share and cooperate with others, and to learn and obey established rules and expectations. Social competency and self-regulation develop as children gain skill in their interactions with peers and adults in new and familiar settings. The quality of children's early relationships with their teachers in child-care facilities is emerging as an important predictor of children's social relations with peers (Howes & Marx, 1992). Both the social and emotional climate of the classroom and the individual relationship between child and teacher can influence the social and emotional development of children.

Implications for Literacy.   Effective teachers understand the importance of establishing a supportive learning environment in which children are encouraged to ask questions and take intellectual risks. Children in this sort of environment are more apt to notice and inquire about print in the environment, and they are likely to attempt reading and writing on their own. They usually will demonstrate a sense of control and self-confidence about their ability to learn.

Cognitive Development

Jean Piaget (1926), B.F. Skinner (1974), and Lev Vygotsky (1984) are among the theorists who have contributed to our thinking about how young children learn. Piaget linked children's intelligence and thinking to the way living organisms organize and adapt to the world around them. According to Piaget, children adapt to new information and experiences in order to maintain a sense of balance. They attempt to make sense of new information by connecting it to what they already know. Skinner relied heavily on the belief that external, environmental forces shape children's behavior. According to Skinner, almost all behavior is learned through experience. Vygotsky focused on the social interaction between children and adults. He was particularly interested in the development of complex thinking. His notion of the **zone of proximal development (ZPD)** has influenced the way many teachers think about teaching. The ZPD is the level at which a child finds a task too difficult to complete alone but achievable with the assistance of an adult or more experienced peer.

Implications for Literacy.   Effective teachers incorporate techniques inspired by all of these theorists. For example, they know that children use their background knowledge, both correctly and incorrectly, to make sense of new information. Such teachers incorporate Piaget's approach as they anticipate difficulties children might have in understanding new concepts and provide the support needed to help children bridge the known to the unknown. Effective teachers also draw from Skinner's work as they break down tasks into incremental steps that systematically reinforce children's behavior and plan instruction that offers children positive reinforcement. The concept of the ZPD has been particularly helpful to teachers in determining how to match instruction with learners' needs. Following Vygotsky's model, teachers determine the best point of entry for teaching and learning and then provide **scaffolding** to move learners toward increasing independence. Thus, children gradually take more and more control of their own learning.

Language Development

From the moment of birth, humans begin learning language, learning about language, and learning through language (Halliday, 1969). Infants and toddlers listen as adults talk and read to them. They learn that listening and talking are pleasant activities. They learn how to take turns talking, how to use language to get what they want, and how to handle a book. By the age of 5 or 6, most children have mastered most of the conventions of oral language. They can produce the sounds in their language, understand many meanings, and use its sentence structures. They have also gained a relatively high degree of communicative competence, the knowledge and use of the social and linguistic rules that govern different situations. For example, their use of language at the dinner table differs from their conversations on the playground. These remarkable accomplishments provide the foundation necessary for language and literacy learning throughout life.

Young children have little difficulty acquiring more than one language. In learning a second language they follow a process similar to that used to acquire the first (Rueda & Garcia, 2002). As with *all* language learning, whether it be the speaker's first or second language, receptive (listening) abilities precede expressive (speaking) abilities. Young children learn the language to which they are exposed.

Implications for Literacy.   Effective teachers are aware that the quality, amount, and kinds of language learning experiences from birth through age 5 have a profound effect on how well children succeed or the extent to which they struggle in their later schooling (Dickinson & Tabors, 2001; Hart & Risley, 1995; Strickland & Barnett, 2003). They adjust their language and their actions in response to what the child needs, responding to a child's intended meaning rather than to a preconceived notion of how that meaning ought to be put into words. They respect and build on the language that children bring to school, whether or not they are native speakers of the language of instruction. Effective teachers expand and support children's language repertoires as a part of their developing social interactions, as well as supporting children's overall intellectual and conceptual development.

Key Principles Shared by the Developmental Domains

Several key principles transcend all the developmental domains. Regardless of the domain, the following principles must be considered, along with what is known about how children grow in each specific developmental area.

Language and culture strongly influence young children's development. Cultural factors influence children's early development profoundly. For example, it is safe to say that children growing up in the print-rich society of the United States are exposed to an abundance of print. Whether it is through books of worship, how-to manuals, television guides, classic literature, or grocery lists, numerous uses of print are demonstrated daily for young children. However, the nature, quality, and number of those experiences will differ from one family to another and from one community to another (Neuman, 1999). Long before formal instruction begins, young children are trying to make sense of their experiences with print. The awareness and understanding they gain, largely through their everyday experiences with adults, are significant and valuable.

Nature and nurture work hand in hand. Children's genes and the environment in which they live determine who they are, how they learn, and how they grow. The environment affects how genes work, and genes determine how we make sense of the world around us. The concept of neural plasticity—the brain's amazing ability to change its structure and function in response to external experiences—helps us understand the impact of both enriched and impoverished environments (Diamond & Hopson, 1999). Environments are not neutral, and a young child's environment, whether at home or at school, is largely determined by adults. Effective teachers and caregivers have a responsibility to provide structure and a well-planned curriculum in which children can learn and grow. In so doing, they must be careful to provide a steady source of emotional support, good nutrition, and an atmosphere free of undue pressure and stress. Children need a broad range of novel learning opportunities and challenges that are neither too easy nor too hard. They should be encouraged to be active participants in their learning, making choices, and interacting with others in a highly social and enjoyable atmosphere.

Children vary in every conceivable way. Although developmental trends apply to all children, individual differences due to genetic and experiential variations and differing cultural and social contexts have strong influences on each child's development. Family and community resources also play a role in these variations. Each child's rate of development may vary as well. Sometimes a child's development will be gradual, cumulative, and continual. At other times, developmental spurts appear to happen within a relatively short period of time. Effective teachers and caregivers expect children to display wide variability in their physical, social, emotional, cognitive, and language skills. They are knowledgeable about the characteristics of the children with whom they work, and they adjust the scope and challenge of the learning opportunities and expectations accordingly (Bowman, Donovan, & Burns, 2000).

Play is essential. Through play, young children learn about their world and gain mastery of their understandings. Play involves language and thinking. It makes physical, social, and emotional demands as well. Children stretch their cognitive abilities as they attempt to solve problems and negotiate the environment during play (Almy, Monighan, Scales, & Van Hoorn, 1984). Recognizing that play is very serious business for young children, effective teachers provide ample time for children to play. They make use of children's tendency to learn through play by providing joyful learning experiences that require just the right amount of challenge.

Motivation to learn is a key factor to school success. Children are active participants in their own learning. Very young children begin to learn about the world through their remarkable capacity to create knowledge from early experience. They seem to be wired to master their world. Environments that provide opportunities and support for growth promote children's natural curiosity and desire to learn.

The developmental domains are interrelated and dynamic. The domains of human development are interdependent. Children in poor health may lack the energy and zest for learning that most young children possess. Children who lack social competence may be reluctant to try new activities or take advantage of available learning opportunities. Similarly, language and cognition are inextricably related. Children's enthusiasm and curiosity about the world motivate them to explore, experiment, and ask an abundance of questions of the adults around them. Environments that are interesting and stimulating and where adults are responsive to children's needs have an enormous impact on what children learn and what they bring to each new learning situation.

All of the developmental domains play a significant role in young children's learning and school readiness. Together, the domains are linked to early learning and later academic achievement and are necessary components of early childhood pedagogy (Bowman et al., 2000). Effective early education programs draw from all the domains of human development and take the child's total development into account, even when focusing on specific aspects of it.

Linking the Developmental Domains With Literacy and School Readiness

In quality early education programs, teachers and caregivers are knowledgeable about the milestones charted in Table 4. Teachers and caregivers can use this knowledge to provide experiences that foster the developmental milestones of language and literacy commonly found in settings where children are afforded rich language and literacy learning opportunities. The experiences may be offered at home, in early education settings, or both. Table 4 provides a useful tool for thinking broadly about the typical development of most children. It can be helpful in matching instructional strategies to children's developmental needs, taking into consideration children's age, maturity, and experience with print.

Table 4
Milestones in Early Language and Literacy Development

Milestones	Prelanguage Birth–12 months	Language Onset 12–24 months	Language Growth 2–3 years	Language Growth and Onset of Metalanguage Awareness 3–4 years	Reading/Literacy 4–5 years
Universal Language Milestones/Capacity	*Language Perception* • Segments and discriminates phonemes in speech stream *Language Production* • Babbling *Motor* • Physical/social growth, including reaching, grasping, and showing, walking *Social* • Joint attention, social pragmatics (e.g., communicative gestures with multiple intents) • Basic conversational structure (vocalizes when adult is silent, silent when adult vocalizes)	*First Words* • First word milestone around 12 months • First 2-word milestone around 18 months • First 50 words around 18–24 months (also true for bilingual children) *Vocabulary* • "Spurt" around 18–22 months (including growth in semantic richness of words)	*Vocabulary Growth* • Plus semantic growth (word meanings) *Phonological* • Production of most sounds of native language *Morphological* (e.g., -s, -ed) • Markings on basic words appear • Onset of over-regularizations (My foots hurt. I goed to the store.) *Syntactic* • Sentence length increases • Growth in phrasal, clausal structure complexity *Storytelling* • Very basic capacity appears	*Vocabulary Growth* • Plus semantic growth *Phonological, Morphological, and Syntactic (Sentence Structure) Growth* • Comprehension and production of more complex syntax, including relative clauses and passive sentences *Rhyming/Word Play* • Word play appears *Narrative Stories* *Conversational*	*Vocabulary Growth* • Later developing phonology refinements and complex syllables, plus semantic growth *Morphological and Syntactic* • Basic morphological and syntactic knowledge now stabilized in native language, with additional "later-syntax" embellishments *Narrative Flourishes* *Conversational*

Table 4 (continued)

Milestones	Prelanguage Birth–12 months	Language Onset 12–24 months	Language Growth 2–3 years	Language Growth and Onset of Metalanguage Awareness 3–4 years	Reading/Literacy 4–5 years
Universal Language Milestones/Capacity (continued)	• Adult vocalization may signal simultaneous child vocalizations		*Conversation* • Structure and pragmatic complexity increase over time		
University Reading/Literacy Milestones/Capacity			*Book Concepts* • Emerging; include shared book reading or social engagement of literacy materials *Print Concepts* • Emerging *Letter Identification* • Emerging *Text Comprehension* • Emerging (books, stories read aloud)	*Book Concepts* • Page-turning, orientation *Print Concepts* • Understanding the concept of a word (word boundaries, which are not evident in speech), letters, sentences, fact that print evokes meaning *Letter Recognition and Naming* • Emerging *Concept of Letter–Sound Correspondence (phonics)* • Emerging *Text Comprehension* • Increasing; more complex texts	*Book Concepts* • Established *Print Concepts* • Established *Letter Recognition and Naming* • Significantly increases *Concept of Letter–Sound Correspondence* • Strengthens *Text Comprehension* • Increases *Reads and Writes Own Name*

Note. Adapted from Petitto and Hirsh-Pasek (2002).

Suggestions for Reflection and Discussion

Does your state, district, or school have preschool standards? If so, what are their expectations for concepts of print, phonemic awareness, and alphabet knowledge, and how are you and your colleagues addressing them? Reflect on your classroom. Discuss the learning opportunities available in each category with your colleagues. Which items do you feel confident about? Which items need more attention? Use Tables 1, 2, and 3 as a guide.

The need to maintain developmentally appropriate practice while addressing accountability often leads educators to take sides between "what is best for children" and "what will further children's ability to demonstrate what they have learned." The discussion tends to dichotomize the way people think about literacy learning and promote misunderstandings about the distinction between what is important to teach and how it should be taught. Is this a point of tension in your school? If so, talk about what it means for helping children learn about print.

Widely accepted best practices in early childhood literacy education suggest that effective early childhood literacy programs

- Are grounded in what is known about children's physical, social, emotional, and cognitive development
- Are planful and intentional
- Acknowledge and value differences among children
- Involve scaffolding children's experiences from the known to the unknown
- Engage children in ways that are meaningful and pleasurable
- Are developmentally appropriate

Read these descriptions and discuss them with your colleagues. What might these practices mean for your program?

Suggestions for Interactive Activities

As you review and discuss the language and literacy standards for your school or district, discuss ways to address them in an integrated way through content of interest to children. Social studies and science content provide an excellent vehicle for expanding children's background knowledge and their language and literacy skills. Try out some of the ideas discussed and share them with others.

Use Table 4 to think and talk about the children you teach. Keeping in mind that these are broad guidelines, are there children whose development is of great concern? You might want to discuss areas where your experience and the chart in Table 4 differ. Share examples of students who tend to be at either end of the spectrum—somewhat delayed in their development or accelerated. Discuss how you meet the challenges of working with diverse populations of all kinds.

Suggestions for Follow-Up

Continue to share examples of focused attention on literacy standards within meaningful, content-rich contexts.

Continue to follow up with the discussion regarding the need to reconcile perceived tension between developmentally appropriate practice and the demands for demonstrated progress. How are you and your colleagues maintaining an atmosphere of enjoyment and engagement in the literacy activities in which children are involved?

CHAPTER 2

Providing a Print-Rich Environment

One important way that children construct knowledge about print is through interactions with logos, labels, road signs, and other meaningful visual displays found in their environment. Children observe as adults use environmental print in functional ways (for example, to choose from a menu, to stop at a stop sign, and to select products at the supermarket). Children who understand how print functions in their lives are more apt to be curious about how written language works. They develop a growing curiosity about words and letters, and they are likely to ask questions about what written words say. Their emerging awareness of how print functions is a key motivating force for learning to read. Sometimes children make use of these meaningful symbols as they choose a particular kind of juice from the refrigerator or return classroom materials to a bin with a picture label. Effective teachers plan the environment so that children are engaged in interpreting and using meaningful symbols. Therefore, this chapter offers suggestions for planning and implementing three important aspects of the classroom environment: (1) materials, (2) print exposure and use, and (3) adult–child interaction.

> Effective teachers plan the environment so that children are engaged in interpreting and using meaningful symbols.

Materials

Careful selection and placement of materials can make a big difference in how well children make use of the environment to learn about print. Materials for reading, drawing, and writing should be available in many areas of the classroom. Materials should allow children to make choices, work independently or with others to complete a task, and develop both creativity and skills. Figure 2 offers a checklist for planning and using materials. Table 5 lists examples of materials and activities that promote children's awareness of shapes, forms, and symbols.

Figure 2
Checklist for Planning and Using Materials

___ Materials are easily accessible and usable by children.

___ Sufficient quantities of materials are available for children's use.

___ Easels and writing areas are organized so that children are encouraged to interact with one another during painting and writing.

___ The writing center is equipped with a variety of supplies: pencils, markers, crayons, and paper of many sizes, shapes, and colors.

___ The computer is equipped with interactive software to encourage children to manipulate letters, draw, follow directions, and use electronic books.

___ A printer is available for children's use.

___ Bulletin boards or pocket charts are used to display daily activities, weekly jobs, or learning center choices.

___ The library center includes class books that have been authored by the group after children have gained enough familiarity through rereading that they can "read" them on their own.

Table 5
Materials and Activities That Promote Awareness of Shapes, Forms, and Symbols

Materials	Activities
• ABC and number books	• Classifying
• Alphabet boards (for matching)	• Comparing
• Alphabet cards	• Differentiating by color, shape, and size
• Board games (lotto, bingo)	• Drawing and writing
• Chalkboards and chalk	• Matching
• Class books	• Pairing
• Dominoes (with pictures for younger children)	• Patterning
• Magnetic letters and magnet boards	• "Reading" and independent browsing
• Assorted paper for writing and drawing	• Sequencing
• Picture dictionaries	
• Pictures of objects to pair, match, and classify	
• Writing utensils	

Print Exposure and Use

It is not enough that children learn to notice print in their environment. They must understand the uses and functions of print in their daily lives, both inside and outside of school. In print-rich classrooms, opportunities for using environmental print emerge throughout the day. In addition, effective teachers plan specific activities to make use of the print to which children are exposed. Some of these activities are embedded in daily routines such as using name cards to take attendance. Other activities result from special experiences. For example, a trip to the firehouse might inspire a chart listing the things children think they might see. Vocabulary words such as *fire engine* might be labeled with pictures so that children begin to associate written words with their meanings. See Figure 3 for guidelines for print exposure and use. Table 6 offers suggestions for how print might be included in various play areas.

Figure 3
Checklist for Print Exposure and Use

___ Print is visible on open charts and bulletin boards around the room.

___ Print is incorporated in each area of the classroom.

___ Environmental print is clear, easy to read, and displayed at children's eye level.

___ Environmental print represents words that are familiar to children because of daily activities, thematic inquiries, and special experiences.

___ Children's names are printed on their cubbies, placemats, and other items.

___ Name cards and other carefully printed words are available for children to copy or "read."

___ Children are encouraged to write their own names or letters from their names on their paintings and drawings.

___ Some print is written in languages other than English.

___ Mailboxes are available for each child and family, encouraging communication between home and school and showing children that written messages are an integral part of classroom life.

___ A newsletter describing children's activities is shared with the children and sent home regularly.

Table 6
Supporting Print Awareness Through Play Areas

Block Area	Office Area	Restaurant Area
• Books and pictures of tools	• Appointment book/calendar	• Cash register
• Catalogs or advertisements from home-supply stores	• File folders	• Chalkboard and chalk
• Markers and cardboard for making signs	• Forms	• Menus
• Pictures of buildings	• Message pads	• Order pads
• Signs and posters reflecting different cultures	• Pens, pencils, markers	• Play money
	• Signs and posters reflecting different cultures	• Signs and posters reflecting different cultures
	• Trays for holding materials	

Adult–Child Interaction

Children's knowledge of print flourishes when they are involved in nurturing relationships with caring and responsible adults. Such adults not only plan opportunities for children to learn about print, but they also take advantage of children's natural curiosity about the print in their environment. They answer children's questions, extend their understanding, and prompt new learning whenever the opportunities occur. Figure 4 offers guidelines for print- and learning-related adult–child interaction.

Figure 4
Checklist of Guidelines for Adult–Child Interaction

___ Adults respond to children's questions about print in positive, supportive ways.

___ Adults model the functions of print so that children are aware of its use.

___ Adults take care to provide inviting displays that include print.

___ Adults offer praise and encouragement when children attempt to read and write.

___ Adults take advantage of "teachable moments" to extend children's knowledge by relating new discoveries to what children already know.

___ Adults are aware that children need time to express their thoughts and ideas.

___ Adults build on what is known about children's linguistic and cultural backgrounds to help them move from the known to the unknown.

Well-planned early literacy programs have structures that allow for **differentiated instruction**; that is, teachers meet with the whole group, with small groups, or with individuals depending on the activity. The younger children are, the more they need one-on-one adult attention, but this will not happen automatically (Schickedanz, 2003). Ironically, programs that have a tightly organized underlying structure are more likely to yield a fluid, comfortable daily schedule for children. This requires considerable forethought and cooperation among staff. Table 7 provides some general guidelines for planning differentiated instruction.

Table 7
Instructional Groupings to Differentiate Instruction

Organizational Pattern	Interactions
Whole Group • Generally occurs once or twice a day; includes read-aloud time, interactive writing, phonological awareness activities, and letter knowledge activities	• Explicit instruction in content to which all children should be exposed • Intentional; builds on stated curriculum goals • Used diagnostically to determine the need for individual and small-group follow-up instruction
Small Group (two to five children) • Generally occurs as part of center-time activities	• Follow-up to whole-group activity • Opportunity to revisit specific aspects of whole-group activity with two or three children (e.g., "Did you notice any letters that looked the same on our chart?") • Intervention for English-language learners, educationally advanced children, and children with other special needs
One on One • May occur during center time or as brief, highly focused adult–child interactions throughout the day	• Same as small-group instruction, only individualized

Suggestions for Reflection and Discussion

Share your daily planning structure with others. Is time for whole-group, small-group, and one-on-one instruction built in? What can you learn from others about dealing with the challenges of differentiated instruction?

Suggestions for Interactive Activities

To promote a more effective discussion of the classroom environment, plan a series of visits to various classrooms. Invite host teachers to lead a tour of what is observed and how it evolved and is used. Share ideas for enriching the environment and effectively using materials.

Suggestions for Follow-Up

Providing the least restrictive environment for children with special needs can be challenging. Throughout the year, make it a point to seek out and share good ideas for working collaboratively with special educators and intervention specialists. Keep in mind that an effective print-rich environment is purposeful, cognitively stimulating, and engaging for all the children in the classroom.

CHAPTER 3

Skills and Strategies: An Overview

In Chapters 1 and 2 we laid out the rationale and framework for helping children learn about print. The remaining chapters focus on what teachers and administrators must do to apply this information. We will address the primary aspects of learning about print—concepts of print, phonemic awareness, and alphabet knowledge. For each aspect, we will introduce an integrated **strategy** that demonstrates how learning about print is embedded within the broader context of instruction, as well as several focused strategies, one of which will be center based. The strategies in Chapters 4–6 will be organized around the following headings: What It Does, How to Do It, Variations, What to Look For, and How to Accommodate Differences. In addition, ideas for home–school connections, assessment (of both children and programs), meeting the needs of diverse learners, and tips for professional development will be offered throughout. First, however, it is important to share two key ideas that are fundamental to the use of all the strategies we offer: the distinction between a skill and a strategy, and the notion of scaffolded instruction.

What Is a Skill? What Is a Strategy?

Skills and strategies are distinct from each other (Paris, Wasik, & Turner, 1991). People perform skills the same way every time (for example, recognizing the names of letters and reading from left to right); therefore, skill instruction is often accomplished through drill and repetition. On the other hand, strategies are plans for solving problems encountered in constructing meaning (Duffy, 1993). Unlike skills, strategies are not automatic. Learners modify their plans or strategies according to the situation. For instance, the pronunciation of the word *read* depends on the meaning of the sentence in which it appears. The reader uses the meaning of the sentence in a strategic way to decide how *read* will be pronounced.

> Unlike skills, strategies are not automatic. Learners modify their plans or strategies according to the situation.

If a young child can recite the alphabet, it is quite an accomplishment, but it is not a strategy. It is a skill. Having that skill does not mean that the child understands that letters are used to form words and that changing the order of the letters actually changes the word. It is very important to keep in mind the distinction between a skill and a strategy, especially when teaching phonemic awareness and alphabet knowledge. Although it is important for children to hear the sounds in words and to name letters, this is only a small part of what they need to know. Both phonemic awareness and letter knowledge may function as isolated skills that are not very helpful unless children understand how to apply them as they read and write. At that point, these skills become useful strategies. This is why teachers must continually model the uses and processes of reading and writing in a variety of formal and informal ways. As children observe how the system of language works, they begin to connect their knowledge of sounds and letters to reading and writing. They begin to ask questions about letters and words. Ultimately, they begin to try out what they know through their own attempts to read and write.

Teachers often think that they must teach skills to mastery level before they can engage children in reading and writing activities. But teachers who immerse children in meaningful activities, in which print is read, written, and discussed, go well beyond helping children learn the letter names and sounds. They help children learn how to use their knowledge of letters and sounds and help them discover the reasons why these skills are important. A teaching strategy called scaffolding assists teachers who want to help children understand how to use the skills they are learning and thus hasten the day when children begin to read and write independently.

What Is Scaffolded Instruction?

Scaffolding refers to the process whereby a child's learning occurs in the context of full performance of a task as adults gradually relinquish support (Cazden, 1988). Think of the phrase "Everybody needs a helping hand," and it will be easy to remember what scaffolding is. As adults, we frequently help children accomplish things they want to do, such as working with a puzzle, writing the first letters of their names, or riding bikes. First, we show them how we do the task. Then, we invite them to try the task, and we help as they attempt to do it. At times we intervene, but only when our assistance is needed. When we think they are ready, we let them try the task on their own. Figure 5 outlines the scaffolding process.

Figure 5
Scaffolding Process

Step 1—Adult controls (teacher does everything)
• Demonstrates/models for children

Step 2—Adult guides (teacher includes children)
• Invites group participation
• Demonstrates with children

Step 3—Adult monitors (teacher observes and helps when needed)
• Invites children to try on their own
• Observes to determine who is successful and who needs additional help

Scaffolded instruction in reading and writing offers teachers opportunities to focus on concepts of print, phonemic awareness, and alphabet knowledge. An example of scaffolding occurs when teachers use Big Books and charts to read aloud to children. When children track the print as teachers read aloud, the children observe the reading process. Although the teacher is doing the reading, the children can follow along mentally as some words are pointed out and as they notice how the reader moves across and down the page and through the book from front to back. After one or two repeated readings of the same book, the teacher may occasionally pause and point to a particular word that has been repeated several times. The children share in the reading by "filling in" that word. If the book is left in the library corner, many children will attempt to "read" it on their own. Thus, a type of scaffolding has occurred in a very informal, relaxed manner. Table 8 depicts one way that teachers might think about the scaffolding process as they plan literacy experiences for children.

Children who are fortunate enough to have books in their homes frequently like to browse among those that have been read to them. No doubt, this is one of the reasons that such children seem to thrive with instruction. Classrooms with an ample supply of books and teachers who read to children on a daily basis can provide the same kind of opportunities. Repeated readings of favorite books often foster the memorization of all or parts of the text. Children may be seen "reading" favorite books to stuffed animals or to each other. This kind of play fosters a love of books and reading. It is of great value for very young children when they are learning various concepts of print, such as page turning, directionality, and the notion that the squiggles on the page evoke what is said. Older children begin to recognize

Table 8
Key Types of Literacy Experiences for Children

Reading Skills/Concepts	Read Aloud	Read Along	Read Alone
• Book handling	(Teacher models and children observe)	(Teacher guides and children participate)	(Teacher monitors and children work independently)
• Concept of word	• Teacher reads aloud, using Big Books or charts, as children observe.	• Teacher reads aloud, using Big Books or charts, as children observe.	• Teacher provides materials and time for children to select books to "read" on their own (see Figure 6).
• Concept of letter			
• Directionality			
• Functions of print			
• Letter names	• Teacher comments aloud about text.	• Teacher invites children to participate at various points during reading.	• Teacher encourages children to talk about their independent reading experiences.
• Language of literacy (e.g., *book, story, title, page, author, illustrator, poem*, etc.)			
• Phonemic awareness			
• Print conveys meaning			

Writing Skills/Concepts	Write Aloud	Write Along	Write Alone
• Concept of word	• Teacher writes and comments aloud as children observe.	• Teacher writes as children observe.	• Teacher provides materials and time for children to draw and write on their own.
• Concept of letter		• Teacher may invite children to suggest letters based on sounds he or she isolates for spelling.	
• Directionality			
• Functions of print	• Teacher may sound out words to spell them or simply spell them aloud.		• Teacher encourages children to share their drawing and writing with others.
• Letter names			
• Language of literacy (e.g., *title, line, beginning, end, letter, word*, etc.)	• Teacher makes other comments about the message.	• Teacher suggests placement of words.	• Teacher is available to assist children.
• Phonemic awareness			
• Print conveys meaning			

words and phrases that are repeated throughout the text. Time set aside when children select their own books and read independently allows them to apply what they have learned through teacher-guided, direct instruction and to enjoy the role of "reader" as they use the illustrations to prompt their recall of the story. Children also have time to inspect the illustrations closely when they look at books independently. Teachers should be mindful that this is an important time of the day and that even independent activities need to be planned and monitored. Table 9 outlines how teachers might plan for independent reading in preschool, and Figure 6 shows students enjoying independent reading time.

Table 9
Independent Reading in Preschool Settings

Before Independent Reading	1. Invite children to gather on the rug.
	2. Involve children in usual group activities such as the following:
	  • Read-aloud and response to literature
	  • Active firsthand experiences and discussion
	  • Phonological and phonemic awareness activities
	  • Group reading and writing activities such as Message time

During Independent Reading	3. Set out books previously read and discussed. (These should be duplicate copies of familiar texts: ABC and number books, other concept books, patterned text, informational books, poetry, Mother Goose stories, and so on.)
	4. Allow children to select books and "read" in pairs or as individuals. They may remain on the rug or find a quiet place in the room to read independently.
	5. Observe children for the following:
	  • Knowledge of text (words and phrases memorized)
	  • Book-handling skills and concepts of print
	  • Phonemic awareness (recall of rhyming words or words with the same beginning sounds)
	  • Alphabet knowledge (comments on or naming of letters in text)

After Independent Reading	6. Call on two or three children to share what they "read." Observe for their use of book language (e.g., *book*, *pictures*, *word*, and *page*) and ability to share concepts and ideas.

Figure 6
Independent Reading Time

Suggestions for Reflection and Discussion

Ask yourself, Do I model, demonstrate, and guide practice to show students how to do something, rather than simply tell them to do it?

Reflect on a typical day in your classroom. Is there a deliberate attempt to meet individual needs through personalized time with children? (Keep in mind that a pair of children constitutes a small group at the preschool level.) Are there some children who dominate the time you have for one-on-one conversation and instruction? Remember that all children need individual attention, but some may appear very independent or may be too shy to call attention to themselves.

Suggestions for Interactive Activities

Observe a demonstration of a lesson that focuses on print concepts. The demonstration may be provided by a fellow teacher or someone leading the professional development effort in your school. It may be done with children, simulated without children, or it may make use of a video that fits with the ideas and strategies offered in the chapter. Keep the chapter content in mind as you participate in a discussion of examples from the demonstration that illustrate understanding about language and literacy development, effective teaching, and connections to your district- or school-based standards and assessment.

Suggestions for Follow-Up

Independent reading time is often treated as a "throw away" time with little or no attention to the possibilities for teaching and learning. By circulating among the children as they peruse books and holding brief conferences with them about their interactions with print, a great deal can be learned about their development. Simply engage a child with a brief discussion about the book he or she is "reading." You might ask the child to tell you about a particular page or about what they have "read" so far. If it is a concept book, such as an alphabet book or a number book, ask the child to tell you about any letters or numbers they know. Use a sticky note to record the date, book title, and any comments you might have. Place the sticky note in the child's portfolio. You may only get to each child once a week or so, and this is fine; the important thing is to hold conferences on a regular basis. This will allow you to note progress and provide documentation to share with parents and others involved with the child's education. See Table 9 for additional ideas.

CHAPTER 4

Strategies for Developing Concepts of Print

A s noted in Chapter 1, the term *concepts of print* refers to knowledge of the functions of print and how print language works. This knowledge requires an understanding of the following:

- The overall structure of book reading and conventions of the printed word
- The fact that print evokes meaning and has a variety of uses in people's lives
- The notion that to make sense of print one needs to understand its directionality (i.e., front to back, top to bottom, and beginning to end)
- The concept of word (i.e., word boundaries and the visual order of letters within a word)
- The concept of letter (i.e., letters have distinct shapes, have names, and form words)

This chapter presents four strategies that support children's concepts of print. The first strategy, **shared writing**, is an integrated instructional strategy. That is, it addresses many concepts of print within a broad activity framework. The additional strategies are narrower activities that focus more specifically on a single print concept. Examples of additional strategies are also given. These focused strategies concentrate on specific aspects of concepts about print and may be used as follow up to whole-group instruction with small groups of children who need additional support. They may also be used for review with the whole group, if needed.

Shared Writing: An Integrated Instructional Strategy

In shared writing, the teacher models the writing process as students observe or participate and respond.

What It Does

Shared writing allows the teacher, a skilled writer, to guide children from thinking and talking to writing. As the teacher thinks aloud about what will be written and how it will be spelled, children witness the way letters, sounds, and words are linked to express ideas in written form. The teacher demonstrates the conventions of print by noting when children need to use a capital letter or a period, for example. Of course, very young children are not expected to know all of this, but they do gain familiarity with the language of literacy: the letter *m*, the end of a word, the beginning of a new sentence, and so on. Shared writing gradually moves to more interactive writing in which the children are encouraged and expected to participate. This progression helps children gain familiarity with the writing process.

How to Do It

1. Start with an inquiry activity in which children are engaged in experiences of interest and importance to them. This may be a hands-on activity, such as planting seeds or caring for a pet, or it may be a literature-based activity, such as a discussion of a book that has been read aloud. Experiences such as these spark children's interest and stimulate language and thinking.

2. Guide children in a discussion about the activity they have experienced or the material they have heard you read. Decide which ideas should be written down, and say to the children, "We can save these ideas by writing them down."

3. To model or demonstrate for the children, you may do a "write-aloud." During a write-aloud, you think aloud as you write, as if you were talking to yourself. For example, say, "Let me see, I think that I will write down the things I need to plant the seeds. I will need some soil. Soil starts with /s/, and we use the letter *s* to stand for /s/. So, I will write the letter *s* first. I know that the other letters are *o*, *i*, and *l*, *s-o-i-l: soil.*" Finish writing the word *soil* and follow the same process to write the other words you will need. The amount written may be several sentences or only one or two words.

   If you wish to involve the children in more interactive shared writing, you might pause at points along the way where you think they might be able to participate. For example, you might say, "I know that the word *soil* starts with /s/, just like Sandra's name. Sandra, do you think you know what letter I need?" Or you might simply wish to have the children call out what they think the letter will be without you offering a word to link it to.

Figure 7 shows one group's shared writing composition. In this example, children's responses to *If You Give a Mouse a Cookie* by Laura Joffe Numeroff (1985) include oral and written language as well as a hands-on activity. Their words and actions are captured through print and then illustrated with photos.

4. A shared writing chart may be completed in one day or in brief segments over a period of several days. When the chart is complete or when the children have done enough for one sitting, guide them in a reading of what has been written. Children can "read" along to the best of their ability. If the writing occurs over several days, it is a good idea to start each new session by rereading what has already been written. This helps reorient the children to the task and their purpose for writing. Then, continue with the new writing and end with a complete rereading of everything.

Figure 7
Sample of Shared Writing in Response to Literature

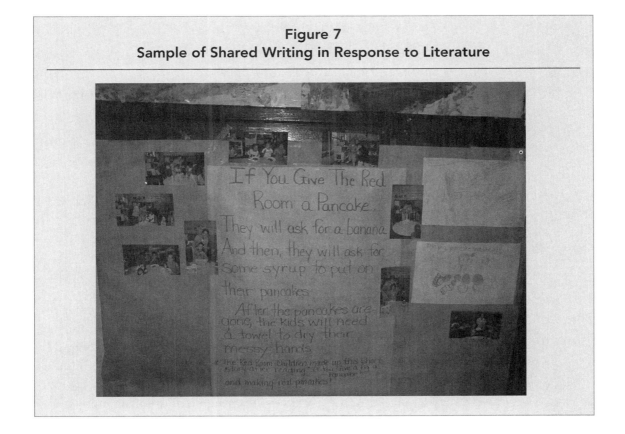

5. Rereading may be followed by a guided discussion of the things children notice about the text. Point to the words and say, for example, "I notice that the word *soil* and the word *seeds* both start with the same letter. That letter is *s*. Does anyone else notice anything they would like to tell us about? Can anyone find the letter *s* somewhere else?" You may have to model this "noticing" process for several weeks before the children catch on. Keep it brief and expect that many children will gradually begin "noticing" with you.

6. Use independent drawing or writing as a follow-up activity for those children who are interested. These compositions may be shared with the class, if the children are willing.

The following list summarizes the ways that teachers can model literacy behaviors and encourage children's involvement during shared writing to support their development of print concepts. The teacher

- Involves children in an activity or discussion that generates a shared experience worth writing about
- Acts as scribe (at the chalkboard or on a chart)
- Thinks aloud about content and language
- Speaks and comments as he or she writes
- Pauses for children to suggest words or letters that might come next
- Guides group reading and rereading
- Guides the analysis of text by discussing ideas and noticing print language patterns (e.g., repeated phrases) and known elements (e.g., letters and words)
- Encourages children to "try out" writing on their own and provides materials and guidance at their request

Variations

Create a Daily Class Journal.   Many teachers keep a class journal in which individual children or the whole class dictates a sentence or two each day. At the end of each week, the teacher punches holes in the new pages so they can be placed with other pages in a class journal bound by three metal rings. Some teachers leave space on each page for children's illustrations. The pages of the class journal may be laminated, and the journal may be placed in the library center, where children can enjoy it as a read-aloud or explore it during independent reading time.

Vary the Forms of Writing. It is important that children are exposed over time to a variety of forms and purposes for writing. Children's names, lists, informal notes, and labels needed in the room are all good content for shared writing.

It is important that children are exposed over time to a variety of forms and purposes for writing.

Vary the Activity for Developmental Appropriateness. Shared writing activities should be adjusted in length and with respect to vocabulary use according to the ages and maturity levels of the children.

What to Look For

Shared writing offers an excellent opportunity to teach concepts of print and to determine which concepts most children have acquired and which require more practice. It is an excellent device for determining the extent of the individual differences within the group as well. Keep in mind that it is as important to determine what children *do* know as it is to learn what they do not know. The observation checklist in Figure 8 can be used both

---

Figure 8
Observation Checklist for Assessing Children's Knowledge of Concepts of Print

Observe children's understanding of the following concepts:

Print Conveys Meaning
___ Writing is a way to express ideas.

Directionality
Speech is written from ___ left to right and ___ top to bottom.

Concept of Word
___ Words are composed of letters.
___ Words match to speech.
___ There are spaces between words.

Letter Knowledge
___ Correct letter names are used.

Phonemic Awareness
___ Some words have the same beginning sounds. (The child is beginning to perceive some relationship between the sounds and letters.)

Literacy Language
___ Certain words (e.g., *word, letter, story, author*) are used to talk about reading and writing.

as a tool during shared writing to assess children's knowledge of print and as a planning guide for future lessons.

How to Accommodate Differences

Accommodations for English-Language Learners. Include in shared writing activities some words in languages other than English whenever feasible. You may need to ask others for spelling assistance, but it is worth the extra effort to demonstrate that languages other than English are valued and that they, too, can be written down.

Accommodations for Atypical Learners. In any group, the children will vary widely in their understanding of what you are attempting to convey through shared writing. At the very least, children need to understand that their thoughts and speech can be written down and that people use letters to form words in order to do this. These fundamental concepts of print underlie the more refined concepts children need to learn in order to read and write. Focus on these big ideas with children who are developing more slowly than others, and then build to more complex concepts.

Accommodations for Advanced Learners. Children who show an interest in independent drawing and writing should be gently guided through the following writing process as they attempt to write on their own.

- *Prewriting*: Help children discuss ideas they want to draw or write about.

- *Drafting*: Encourage children to draw about their ideas and write something to accompany their drawings. Encourage them to use what they know about letters and sounds as they write. Follow the children's lead. Offer assistance if you hear a child attempting to sound out a word, perhaps by repeating it softly. Answer children's questions about spelling but avoid pushing them beyond their interest or ability levels.

- *Revising*: When a child is finished drawing or writing, ask, "Is your picture/story just the way you want it to be?" Get children in the habit of looking over what they have done. Most often they will say it is fine. Now and then, they may want to add something.

- *Sharing*: During sharing time, invite children to talk about their pictures and "read" what they have written. Children may share individual writing with the teacher, individual peers, or the whole class.

This process may be used with all children. However, it is important to follow the child's lead and provide instruction according to each child's needs.

Focused Strategy 1: Things I Like

Children collect pictures of things they like, such as food or hobbies. These are pasted on paper and labeled by the teacher.

What It Does

This strategy supports children's understanding that speech can be written down and supports their development of concept of word and concept of letter.

How to Do It

You will need old magazines, scissors, glue or paste, and 8½ 3 11-inch pieces of paper.

1. Provide a generous supply of pictures cut from magazines or other sources. You will need at least three or four per child.

2. Print the words "Things I Like" at the top of a large piece of paper for each child. Ask the children to choose three pictures of things they like. Assist them in pasting the pictures on the paper.

3. Have each child name aloud each item in the pictures he or she selected. Write the name of each item next to its picture, saying aloud the letters as you write.

4. When the writing is complete, read the words again, pointing to each word and encouraging the child to join in.

Variations

Vary the Theme. You may wish to change the theme of the picture collection (for example, "Toys I Like" or "Animals I Like").

Find a Word. When the writing is complete, use a separate sheet of paper to write down one of the words. Ask the child to find that word on his or her paper.

Find a Letter. When the writing is complete, use a separate sheet of paper to write down a letter from one of the words. Name the letter and ask the child to find that letter in other words.

What to Look For

Look for the child's ability to name the pictures he or she has collected. This is an opportunity to develop the child's vocabulary. If a child offers a word other than the word you expect, either offer the "correct" word or suggest that the item may be called by more than one name. In the latter case, always write the word the child gives.

Look for the child's ability to match words and letters. When children match words, encourage them to look at *all* the letters (not just the first letter) to see that the words are exactly alike.

How to Accommodate Differences

Accommodations for English-Language Learners. Whenever possible, inquire about what something is called in the language the child speaks at home and write the word in both English and the child's home language. If you are unsure of how the word is spelled in the child's home language, simply have the child say the word for you and do not attempt to write it.

Accommodations for Atypical Learners. For the child who is developing more slowly than most, point out how symbols stand for things. For example, touch the chair the child is sitting on and say, "This is a real chair that you are sitting on right now." Show a picture of a chair and say, "Here is a picture of a chair." Write the word *chair* and say, "This is the word that stands for chair, and we can read it and write it. This is the word *chair*."

Accommodations for Advanced Learners. After writing a word, you might ask, "Do you see any letters you know?" Say a word and then ask, "Can you tell me how that word sounds at the very beginning?" Choose only the beginning sounds that you think the child might be familiar with, and provide plenty of support.

Focused Strategy 2: Room Word Search

This strategy requires children to search for particular words in the classroom.

What It Does

Engaging children in a room word search encourages them to notice the environmental print around them and offers them an opportunity to discuss the words and their uses in the classroom.

Engaging children in a room word search encourages them to notice the environmental print around them and offers them an opportunity to discuss the words and their uses in the classroom.

How to Do It

1. This might be the final activity during large-group time. Say to the children, "I am going to show you a word that is somewhere in this room. It is the word *crayons*. I will spell it." Point to the letters in the word as you say them and then say the word once again. Ask, "Who would like to see if they can find the word?" Use meaning prompts to help them think critically: "Where do you think the word *crayons* might be found in our classroom?"

2. Select two children, give them a copy of the word, and ask them to search for another example of the word somewhere in the room. When they have found the word, all the other children may gather around to see if it is the correct choice. Ask, "Are the two words the same?" Then say, "Let's look closely and spell it again. Let's look at the first letter. It is the letter *c*. Do both words start with the letter *c*?" Continue with the other letters until everyone agrees that the words are the same, not different. Use the terms *same* and *different* whenever possible because these words are constantly used in literacy instruction.

3. Repeat this process with one or two more words, giving other children a chance to do the search.

4. When appropriate, talk about how the chosen word is useful in the classroom: "The word *crayons* helps us know that our crayons are kept in this tub."

Variations

Use Small Groups.　After demonstrating the activity with the whole class, you might want to work with only two or three children each day, allowing sufficient time to engage them in extended conversation.

Search Charts or Big Books.　Have children search for words on a chart that the class has created or in a Big Book that has been read aloud several times.

What to Look For

Look for children's ability to think about the appropriate location in the classroom where a word might be found. Notice whether or not they look beyond the first letter when two words begin with the same letter. Listen to hear which children follow along as you spell aloud.

How to Accommodate Differences

Accommodations for English-Language Learners. In cases where you have labels written in two languages, use one or the other, and identify the language for the children. State and spell the word and say, "See if you can find it."

Accommodations for Atypical Learners. Choose very obvious words for children who are just beginning to get the idea that the same word can be written down in more than one place. Stress how the words function in the classroom. Use words that have meaning for the child, such as familiar names, labels in the room, and words that have appeared over and over again in charts created through shared writing. Too often, learning is made very rote for these children and lacks an appreciation that all children need meaningful opportunities to develop genuine understanding.

Accommodations for Advanced Learners. Some children will have already demonstrated an interest in the words in the environment by asking questions about them and attempting to read them on their own. Use the room word search similarly with them, but ask them to try it without taking the word card with them unless they need it. After they think they have found the word, they may use the word card to double-check it. This is a good visual memory activity.

Focused Strategy 3: Building Words

This strategy requires children to reconstruct familiar words, phrases, and sentences. After this activity is modeled with the whole group, the materials may be placed in a learning center where children can do the activity individually or in pairs.

What It Does

This strategy requires that children look at parts within a whole. They learn that word and letter orders are important and that English words and letters are arranged from left to right.

How to Do It

1. You will need two identical copies of the words, phrases, or very short sentences you plan to use. One copy should be left as is to serve as a model; the other should be cut into letters or words. Place all the pieces in a plastic bag.

2. Have children dump out the contents of the bag and attempt to reconstruct the cut-up pieces to match the model copy.

3. Children should only work with words, phrases, and sentences with which they are very familiar. For example, you might select a word that is repeated several times on a class chart. After repeated readings of a Big Book with patterned text, select a short phrase or sentence that the children have joined in to read along with you. For example, use "I think I can," "Jump, Frog, Jump!" or "He was still hungry."

Variations

Use a Child-Created Sentence.   Ask a child to dictate a sentence. Write it down and make a duplicate copy. Cut out one copy and have the child reconstruct the sentence he or she has dictated. This variation introduces the idea that each printed word stands for a spoken word. Children will also begin to see that printed words have spaces between them, unlike spoken words, which run together as people say them aloud.

What to Look For

This strategy presents an excellent opportunity for children to problem solve and self-correct. Look for children's self-monitoring abilities. Ask children to leave their matching game in the center so that you can see it when it is finished. Guide them as they self-correct their work. Say, "Let's look at what you have done. Do the two sheets of paper look exactly the same? Let's check it out together."

How to Accommodate Differences

Accommodations for English-Language Learners.   This activity can be done in any language. When demonstrating before the whole class, use at least one word or phrase in a language other than English.

Accommodations for Atypical Learners.   Reconstructing sentences and phrases may be confusing for the child who is developing more slowly than most. Concentrate on the child's name first. Then move on to two-word phrases. Working one-on-one with a child offers a good opportunity to notice and follow up on problems that may be vision related.

Accommodations for Advanced Learners.   Stress reconstruction of dictation with children who are on the brink of writing on their own. Point out the spaces between the words. Have children choose a word from a sentence or phrase and spell it while pointing to the letters. Encourage them to try out writing on their own. Notice how they are gaining control over written language and demonstrating what they know. Figure 9 shows a child's dictated version of a picture story.

Assessing Children's Print Awareness
The Print Awareness and Book-Handling Assessment Checklist in Figure 10 is based on the work of Marie Clay (1979) and should be administered

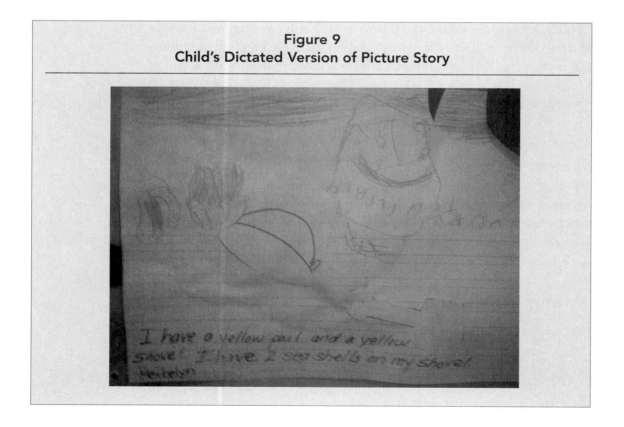

Figure 9
Child's Dictated Version of Picture Story

Figure 10
Print Awareness and Book-Handling Assessment Checklist

Instructions: Administer to one child at a time with a familiar book. You may also observe for these concepts during group activities.

Book Handling

1. ___ What would you need if you wanted me to read a story to you?
2. ___ (Show a book.) What do you do with this?
3. ___ Show me the front of the book.
4. ___ Show me a page in the book.
5. ___ Where should I start reading it?
6. ___ (Show the beginning of a line.) If I start here, which way do I go when I read?
7. ___ Where is the top of the page?
8. ___ Where is the bottom of the page?

Print Awareness

9. ___ Can you show me a word on the page?
10. ___ Can you show me a letter?
     a. Uppercase (capital)?
     b. Lowercase (small)?
11. ___ (Show a scribble.) Is this a word?
12. ___ (Show a well-known logo such as McDonald's or Coca Cola.)
     a. What does this tell about?
     b. Where does it say _____ ?
     c. Are you reading that?
     d. (Print the word.) What does this say?

individually. However, much of this information can be gleaned as you observe children during independent reading time. You may want to reserve individual administration of the assessment for those children about whom you have questions. They may be developing much more slowly or much more rapidly than expected, or they may simply be perplexed.

Making Connections Between Home and School

Use the information in Figure 11 to create your own flier to be sent home to parents or for use at a parents' meeting. Prepare the flier in more than one language, if necessary.

Figure 11
Information for Parents: Learning About Books and Print

We are learning about books and print. Your child is learning the following concepts:
• The print around us has meaning.
• When we think and talk about the things we do, what we say can be written down and read back to us. The print tells the reader what to say.
• Reading and writing let people do many things such as enjoy a story, read a menu, or write a note.

Learning about books and print is important for many reasons:
• The more children know about how print works, the more they will be eager and ready to learn to read.
• They will possess knowledge of basic concepts required for reading and writing.

Here are some ways that you can help:
• Read to your child and encourage him or her to browse independently through books that you have read aloud.
• Show the ways that you use reading and writing in your daily life: writing notes and grocery lists; reading books, magazines, and newspapers; or using the phone book.

SUGGESTIONS FOR REFLECTION AND DISCUSSION, INTERACTIVE ACTIVITIES, AND FOLLOW-UP

Suggestions for Reflection and Discussion
Discuss the strategies offered in this chapter. In what ways are they similar to or different from things you are already doing? Discuss any changes you might make to your curriculum.

Suggestions for Interactive Activities
Observe a demonstration of a lesson that focuses on phonemic awareness. The demonstration may be provided by a fellow teacher or someone leading the professional development effort in your school. It may be done with children, simulated without children, or it may make use of a video that fits with the ideas and strategies offered in the chapter. Keep the chapter content in mind as you participate in a discussion of examples from the demonstration that illustrate understanding about language and literacy development, effective teaching, and connections to your district or school-based standards and assessment.

Suggestions for Follow-Up

Use the checklist in Figure 10 for periodic, informal assessment of children. Discuss with colleagues any children about whom you are concerned or perplexed. Use the information collected on the form as documentation of your assessment of a particular child and as a springboard for discussion.

CHAPTER 5

Phonemic Awareness: Moving From Oral Language to Beginning Links With Print

As noted in Chapter 1, phonemic awareness is the ability to hear, identify, and manipulate the individual sounds (phonemes) in spoken words. It is one aspect or type of phonological awareness, the understanding that words are made up of speech sounds, or phonemes. Activities that boost phonemic awareness build on the broad aspects of phonological awareness, such as identifying and making oral rhymes and clapping out syllables in spoken words. However, phonemic awareness requires narrower and more advanced skills than rhyming and clapping syllables, and it links more directly to phonics, which relates sounds to the letters that represent them. Indeed, instruction in phonemic awareness may involve the use of print.

This chapter presents four strategies that help support children's phonemic awareness. The first strategy, **shared reading**, is a broad, integrated instructional strategy designed to serve as a model for the kind of activities that teachers should use throughout the year. It addresses phonemic awareness as well as a broad range of literacy skills. The additional phonemic awareness strategies progress in difficulty from strictly oral strategies to strategies that begin to link phonemic awareness with print. Examples of additional strategies are also given. These focused strategies concentrate on specific aspects of phonemic awareness and may be used as follow up to whole-group instruction with small groups of children who need additional support. They may also be used for review with the whole group, if needed.

Shared Reading: An Integrated Instructional Strategy

Shared reading involves activities in which the teacher reads aloud to children from materials that allow the children to see the print during the read-aloud. In preschool, the materials are generally Big Books or charts. The teacher models the reading process as children observe or participate and respond.

What It Does

> Books for young children that are rich in rhyming and alliteration are ideal for beginning phonological awareness activities.

Books for young children that are rich in rhyming and alliteration are ideal for beginning phonological awareness activities. Many are available as Big Books, designed for reading in a group setting, where children can see the written words that represent speech. Big Books provide an excellent means of supporting children's knowledge about print. They can provide an informal bridge from phonological awareness to phonemic awareness to print awareness.

In the following strategy, Big Books are used effectively in a whole/part/whole framework (Strickland, 1998) that allows children to experience a whole text before they look at the parts for explicit study. It also allows children to develop a context for using the skills they are learning. Rather than teaching skills in isolation, the whole/part/whole strategy introduces skills in combination with the strategies that utilize them.

There is no doubt that purely oral phonological awareness activities are foundational for reading and writing. However, activities that involve print can also be introduced, providing a playful, yet effective, way for children to simultaneously hear speech patterns and see how they are represented. This integrated strategy demonstrates how the instructional use of Big Books can extend beyond modeling the reading process. Repeated readings provide opportunities for children to listen to fluent reading, learn the language of print, and memorize text. Memorizing text leads children to "read" independently and begin to ask questions about the words on the page.

How to Do It

1. Prepare for the reading. Prepare by reading the Big Book to yourself, preferably several times, before sharing it with the children. Note aspects of the book that provide teaching opportunities, such as alliteration, repeated words, or phrases that enable children to "share" in the reading or match the text with word or phrase strips. Construct a mental and written plan for how you might use it to help children learn about print. You might attach sticky notes to specific pages to remind yourself of prospective teaching points.

2. Introduce the book. Start the first reading by reading the title (while underlining it with your finger) and the names of the author and illustrator. If the cover provides clues about the story, ask a question, such as, "Now that you know the title and you can see the cover, what do you think this book might be about?" This question helps children learn to make predictions. Accept two or three responses. Always ask, "What made you think so?" This question requires children to give an explanation for their answers and discourages random guessing. It is an informal way of introducing young children to the idea that their responses should make sense.

3. Read the book aloud, holding it with the text facing the children so that they have a full view, as illustrated in Figure 12. Avoid tracking the print with your hands or a pointer, particularly during the first reading. Pointing too soon interferes with the children's ability to see the illustrations, which are integral to the text. It may also spoil the phrasing of the language in the book.

Figure 12
Shared Reading With Enlarged Text

4. Through skillful questioning, focus on comprehension and interpretation. For example, consider a sample lesson using *I Went Walking* (Williams, 1989). This book lends itself to prediction questions throughout because the illustrator gives visual clues about the story's events. The children can use these clues to guess what will happen next and then confirm their predictions as the next page is revealed. The book has a patterned text with two lines that are repeated throughout. For *I Went Walking*, the logical comprehension focus would be *making predictions*.

5. Engage children in varied responses. The second and third readings of the text should involve the children in multiple forms of response, such as drama or shared writing. The first reading involved oral language response focused on comprehension. Each subsequent reading should start with a full reading of the text followed by some form of response. Because *I Went Walking* has a repetitive quality and involves a number of animals, you might select a few children to act out the text as you read it aloud. The story is very simple: The main character goes walking, and each animal in the book joins him one at a time. Assign each child an animal character and one child as the main character. As you read the story, have the children listen for the names of their animals and join the others in marching around the room. Provide help as needed.

   To begin a shared writing activity, ask the children if they can recall some of the animals in the story. List the animals on a chart, and act as the scribe as children make suggestions. Prompt children's attention to print by thinking aloud: "*Green duck*. How many words is that? I wonder how the word *green* will start. I think I need a space between the words *green* and *duck*. I want to write *brown horse* on the next line. Where do I start?" Of course, you will need to use questions that make sense for your class. For example, you might write *green duck* and then say, "I needed two words, *green* and *duck*, and I put a space in between each of them so that you could see each word." If the book is short (less than 10 minutes), it may be reread after the response activity. Once the children are familiar with the text, you may want to occasionally select specific parts and track the print with your hand or with a pointer to indicate directionality.

6. Explore print features. After the children have gained familiarity with the book, you may wish to explore some of its print features during subsequent readings. Pace the activities according to the children's responses, and remember that this process should take place over time (perhaps two to four weeks), with a variety of other read-aloud books, charts, and

Big Books. The following list offers suggestions for explaining print features through matching sentences, words, and letters, respectively.

- *Matching Sentences*: Remind children that several times during the past few weeks you have enjoyed this book with them. Today they are going to do something very special. On a piece of oaktag, write two sentences or phrases from the book that are repeated often. Read them aloud to the children. Open the book to a page where one of the sentences or phrases is written. Ask the children to choose the phrase or sentence that matches the one in the book. Keep in mind that the children are not asked to read the sentence or phrase. They are simply matching it visually. Also remember that this may be challenging for some children. Give plenty of support. Point out the length of the phrase or sentence, the way it looks at the beginning and end, the spaces between words, and so on. The objective is to help children notice print more closely than they might have before.

- *Matching Words*: As the children watch, cut one of the sentences or phrases matched above into its individual words. Have the children look at the sentence or phrase in the book and reconstruct it.

- *Matching Letters*: Choose words that look and sound alike at the beginning, write them on cards, and have children find them in the book. Be sure that you read aloud the word on the card as you present it. For example, in *I Went Walking*, the words *went*, *walking*, and *what* are repeated many times. Once the children visually match the words on the cards to those in the book, read the words again, stressing the initial sound and noting how they look and sound alike at the beginning. Also, point out that all start with the letter *w*.

The following list summarizes the ways in which teachers can support children's development of print concepts during shared reading. In shared reading, the teacher

- Selects texts that lend themselves to repetition of phrases, sentences, and sound–symbol relationships
- Allows for a variety of types of response to the same text, including discussion, drama, and shared writing
- Allows for multiple ways to explore the features of print, such as visually matching sentences, words, and letters and reconstructing sentences and words

- Supports connections of phonemic awareness to print (e.g., rhyming and alliteration)
- Models directionality (left to right, return sweep, and top to bottom)
- Encourages the use of the language of literacy (e.g., *book*, *beginning/ end of story*, *page*, *top/bottom of page*, *letter*, *word*, and *sentence*)

Note: It is essential to familiarize yourself with each Big Book and select activities that are appropriate for the particular text and for the children in your class.

Variations

Share Poetry. Teachers often share poetry and song charts with children, and young children quickly memorize the words after several weeks of verbal practice. You can use these materials and point to the words as they are "read" or sung. Once children are very familiar with a particular poem or song, point out some of the words that start with the same sound. For example, after several readings of *Higglety Pigglety Pop!* (Sendak, 1979), you might point out that the words *pigglety*, *pop*, and *pig* all sound alike at the beginning and all start with the letter *p*. After noting the similarity between the way these words sound and look, you might say another word, such as *park*, and ask the children whether they think *park* begins like *pigglety*, *pop*, and *pig* and whether they think it would also begin with *p*. When everyone agrees that it does begin with *p*, then write the word on the board so the children can see it for themselves. Do this with one or two other such words.

Remember that your purpose is to help children link the beginning sounds of words they have learned orally to the visual representations of those sounds (i.e., phonemic awareness linked to print). In this kind of activity, it is not important that children learn any specific sound–symbol relationship. Instead, it is important that they begin to understand the alphabetic principle—that there is a relationship between the individual sounds in words and the letters that represent those sounds. You should vary the forms of text in which you look for these relationships.

What to Look For

Obviously, shared reading provides teachers with opportunities to address a number of aspects of learning about print. The model described previously scaffolds children's learning from broad awareness of print, such as the awareness that print carries meaning and signals what people say when they read, to the finer aspects of textual features and phonemic awareness, such

Figure 13
Observation Checklist for Assessing Children's Knowledge
of Concepts of Print During Shared Reading

Observe children's understanding of the following concepts:

Book Concepts

____ Books have titles, authors, and illustrators.

Print Conveys Meaning

____ Print carries a message.
____ Illustrations carry meaning but cannot be read.

Directionality

Print is read from ____ left to right and from ____ top to bottom.

Concept of Word

____ Words match speech.
____ Words are composed of letters.
____ There are spaces between words.

Letter Knowledge

____ Letters in words can be identified and named.

Phonemic Awareness

____ Some words sound the same at the beginning.
____ The sounds in words are represented by letters.

Literacy Language

____ Certain words (*book, title, author, illustrator, sentence, word, letter,* etc.) help people to talk about what they read.

as the idea that individual letters make up words. Some children will require many such experiences before they begin to understand the relationships between the words they hear as you read aloud and the words and letters printed on the page. Look for children's growing abilities to apply what they know about phonemic awareness and link that knowledge to print. The checklist in Figure 13 can serve as an instructional planning guide.

How to Accommodate Differences

Accommodations for English-Language Learners. Tabors (1998) offers five strategies for use with English-language learners in early childhood settings:

1. Use lots of nonverbal communication.

2. Keep the message simple.

3. Talk about the here and now.

4. Emphasize the important words in a sentence.

5. Combine gestures with talk. (p. 25)

These suggestions are useful for working with any young child and are particularly important when the language of instruction at school is other than the language spoken at home.

Accommodations for Atypical Learners.   All children benefit from opportunities to return to familiar books on their own. Many 3- and 4-year-olds actually memorize parts of books that have been read over and over to them. Providing little-book versions of the Big Books read at school can help this memorization take place. Little books can also be sent home in plastic bags for sharing with members of the family. For the child who is developing more slowly than most, books for promoting phonemic awareness should be read several times at school before they are sent home. Bringing home a familiar book builds a child's confidence because he or she can share the book with family members, listen and participate as the book is read aloud, and talk about the story.

Accommodations for Advanced Learners.   Whenever possible, provide small copies of the Big Books you share with children. These "little books" are often packaged in sets of six. Encourage your advanced learners to "read" the books on their own. You will find that they will be the first to memorize whole texts and to ask about specific words, phrases, and letters.

Focused Strategy 1: Clapping Our Names

This strategy requires children to clap the number of parts (syllables) in their names (Yopp & Yopp, 2000).

What It Does

Clapping the number of parts in a name requires that children listen carefully to separate the syllables they hear. This is not something that children naturally listen for or do on their own. This activity introduces children to the important concept that some words have more than one part and that these parts (syllables) can be counted.

How to Do It

1. Tell children that you have been thinking about their names and how they sound: "Some names, such as *John*, have only one part or syllable. When I think of *John*, I think of clapping one time." Then, say the name *John* and clap once. Repeat. "Other names, such as *Ki-ki* (Kiki), have two parts. So when I think of *Ki-ki*, I clap two times." Say the name *Kiki* and clap two times. Repeat.

2. After demonstrating with a few more names, invite the children to clap some names with you, as illustrated in Figure 14. Begin by using only one- and two-syllable names. When you think the children have caught on, advance to names with more than two syllables. Continue with this phonemic awareness activity as a brief part of large-group time. When most children are capable of listening to and clapping the parts of names, in particular their own, you might want to show a printed name after it has been clapped. The children will learn that they can say it, clap it, and read it.

3. Engage children in making a class book. You will need a sheet of paper for each child, some small scraps of colored paper, and some paste or

**Figure 14
Clapping Our Names**

Figure 15
Class Book: Clapping Our Names

glue. Invite the children to each draw a self-portrait on a separate sheet of paper. Have the children sign their drawings. Then ask each child to say his or her name aloud, count the syllables, and select one paper scrap for each syllable. Have the children paste the paper scraps on their self-portrait pages. Compile the pages into a class book (see Figure 15). Read the book with the children during large-group time; then place it in the library center for children's independent exploration.

Variation

Clapping Other Words.   To help children discover that they can clap the syllables for any word they know, select a word or two from a shared writing exercise. Have the children clap the syllables.

What to Look For

Look for children's ability to attend to the parts they hear in their names and to clap the number of syllables. Continue to model the process and offer many opportunities to listen and clap with the group before asking a child to do it alone.

How to Accommodate Differences

Accommodations for English-Language Learners.   Clapping names or words may be done in any language. Try clapping syllables for names and words in the children's home languages other than English.

Accommodations for Atypical Learners.   Most children can learn this activity fairly easily. Nevertheless, some children have considerable difficulty attending to any level of sounds in words. Clapping names is a good activity for informal screening of such difficulties. After several lessons, notice which children still seem to have difficulty. Find a quiet place and spend a brief time with them one-on-one. You may find that these children are confused by all the clapping or do not understand the directions. They may have problems listening attentively or separating syllables. They may be confused because they are mispronouncing a word. Try to determine where the problem lies. Children may need to work one-on-one with a teacher several times before they fully understand the activity.

Accommodations for Advanced Learners.   Advanced learners will begin to notice that some words are long and are likely to have more syllables. Try having them read a few pages of the class book with you. Cover the paper scraps pasted on each page. If necessary, help the children to read the name. Then ask the children to count and clap the number of parts in it. Finally, show them the pieces of paper pasted on the page to check their work. Keep in mind that it is not necessary for the children to be able to read the names. You can read the names and have the children listen for the number of syllables.

Focused Strategy 2: Matching Beginning Sounds

What It Does

Children learn to listen to the sounds at the beginnings of words and to categorize words according to their beginning sounds. This activity is a precursor to the center-based activity that follows.

How to Do It

1. Ask children to listen to several words that begin with the same sound (e.g., *Sam*, *sip*, and *sock*). Repeat the words, emphasizing the beginning sound. Point out that all of these words begin with the same sound, /s/. Then repeat the words once again.

2. Tell the children that you are going to say another word and think about whether or not it begins like *Sam*, *sip*, and *sock*. Say, "The word I am thinking of is *sick*. Let me see. Does it start like *Sam*, *sip*, and *sock*? Yes, it does. Now I am going to try another word." Continue with other words, such as *sale*, *summer*, and *seal*. Each time go back and say the keywords, *Sam*, *sip*, and *sock*, and then the new word. After modeling two or three times, invite the children to participate. Try at least one word that does not begin with /s/.

3. Play the game for a second or third time, on subsequent days. Modeling for the children, say, "We know these words sound the same at the beginning. I wonder how they look at the beginning. I will write them down to take a look." Write the words *Sam*, *sip*, and *sock* on a chalkboard or chart paper, stressing the sound of the letter *s*. Have the children "read" the words with you. Guide them in noticing that the words all look the same at the beginning. The letter they begin with is the letter *s*. Point out that *Sam* begins with the uppercase *S* and *sip* and *sock* with the lowercase *s*, but they all begin with the same letter.

4. It is important to teach only one letter and its corresponding sound at a time. Instruction should be very brief, simple, and easy for most children to grasp. Keep in mind that the objective of this activity extends beyond learning about the sound–symbol relationship of /s/. The larger goal is to have children understand something about how English works—that sounds in words can be written with letters. Once they realize that there are sound–symbol relationships, they can generalize this idea to match other letters with sounds.

Variations

Match Beginning Sounds Using Pictures.   When most children seem to understand how sounds and letters go together, try this variation. Cut pictures from magazines or draw simple pictures of familiar objects. Paste a picture of an object whose name begins with the target sound at the top of a piece of chart paper. Write the name of the object next to it. For example, draw a picture of a sock and write the word *sock* next to it. One at a time, show the pictures and have children decide whether or not the objects' names begin with the same sound as *sock*. If so, the objects can be pasted on the chart. Note that objects are often called by many names (e.g., *bucket* vs. *pail*; *carton* vs. *box*; *bag* vs. *sack*). You may need to guide children to name the word you have in mind.

Some sound–letter relationships appear to be easier to learn than others. For instance, children usually find it easy to link letter names and sounds when the name of the letter contains the sound (e.g., *b*, *m*, *p*, *s*, and *t*).

Make sure that the words you choose begin with single consonant sounds. Avoid words that begin with consonant blends and digraphs. The beginning sounds of these words cannot be linked to a single letter. Here are some sample word sets to get you started: *bake*, *bug*, and *boat*; *mop*, *milk*, and *make*; *top*, *toes*, and *tent*.

What to Look For

Listen for children's ability to listen and attend to similarities and differences in what they hear. When you say a word, be sure to emphasize the initial sound so that children understand what you mean by the sound at the very beginning of the word. During shared writing, look for children's ability to "assist" in the spelling of sounds. For example, do children attempt to say the first sound separately and think of a letter name to write?

> Listen for children's ability to listen and attend to similarities and differences in what they hear. When you say a word, be sure to emphasize the initial sound so that children understand what you mean by the sound at the very beginning of the word.

How to Accommodate Differences

Accommodations for English-Language Learners.   Assuming that English is the language of instruction, it is important that children pronounce the words in standard English if they are to make the correct sound–letter match. Speak clearly and distinctly as you introduce English words and sounds, and have the children repeat after you. Although this kind of lesson can be applied to any alphabetic language, sound–letter correspondence does vary among languages. For preschool children, stick to simple English sound–letter relationships so that children understand the principle involved.

Accommodations for Atypical Learners.   Sound–letter correspondence is a challenging concept for some children. For some, the issue is time. Atypical learners need more time than most children to grasp concepts and apply them successfully. Individual and small-group activities will help keep them from falling far behind. Keep in mind that the lower your student-to-teacher ratio, the more likely you are to capture and keep children's attention.

Accommodations for Advanced Learners.   Many children who are advanced learners seem to figure out sound–letter correspondence independently. They tend to see patterns more easily than other children. They discover, either on their own or by having someone point it out, that some words share the same beginning sound and that these words also share the same beginning letters. For instance, Billy figures out that *ball* and *basket* have the same beginning sound as his name, and he learns that all three words begin with the letter *b*. He gradually discovers a similar pattern with other sounds and letters. After many formal experiences with print, children like Billy begin to experiment with what they know. These early experiments often take the form of **invented spelling**.

Figure 16 is a self-portrait by a child who is demonstrating awareness of beginning letter sounds. She labeled it with the letters *B* and *D* and read, "My bike and doll" and then explained that the picture shows her playing with her bike and doll. Children with this level of skill benefit from encouragement (but not pressure) to use what they know in their attempts at reading and writing.

Focused Strategy 3: Sorting Picture Cards

Children apply their knowledge of beginning sounds to sort pictures. This strategy should follow an abundance of whole- and small-group activities of the type described in the previous strategy. By observing children in group activities, you will be able to determine when individual children are ready to move into independent work in learning centers.

What It Does

This strategy strengthens children's ability to distinguish the initial sounds in words and reinforces their understanding of the connection between sounds and letters.

How to Do It

1. Before helping children sort pictures according to initial sound, you need to help them understand what sorting is all about. You will need

Figure 16
My Bike and Doll

pictures of items in several categories such as clothes, toys, and animals. These pictures can be drawn or found in books dealing with word study (e.g., Bear, Invernizzi, Templeton, & Johnston, 2000). When introducing picture-card sorting, it helps to designate one picture as a key picture that represents the category. For instance, if children are to sort pictures of clothing, you might draw a dress on red paper and draw the remaining clothing items on white paper. Children can then group the pictures of clothing with the dress. You will also need additional pictures that represent the beginning sounds that you have studied. For example, for the letter *b*, you might use a key picture of a ball. Other pictures might include a bat, a bone, a boy, and a bee.

2. Introduce this activity by modeling the concept of sorting, using categories familiar to the children. For example, you might select clothing and toys. Attach a picture representing each category to the top of a two-column chart, using double-sided tape. Scramble the remaining items on a tabletop. Point out the two pictures on the chart and ask the children to tell you which is a toy and which is a piece of clothing. Explain that there are several pictures in the pile on the table and you are going to sort them according to whether they are clothes, toys, or something else. Hold up the first item and think aloud, "This is a doll. It is a toy, so I will stick it under the toy on the chart." Invite the children to help you sort the remaining pictures. Depending on the group, you might want to practice concept sorting with other common categories (such as food, things used for travel, or animals) before you introduce sorting by sounds.

3. When most of the children have a good understanding of how a sorting game is played, model sorting familiar picture cards according to initial sound. Remind the children that they have been sorting lots of things they know, both as a group and independently in learning centers. This time, instead of paying attention to what category the picture belongs to, they will need to pay attention to the first sound in the name of the object.

4. Demonstrate the process using a sound you have already discussed. Place the pictures for sorting in a plastic bag or an envelope. Dump them on a table and spread them out so that they can be seen easily. At first, it is a good idea to have all but one of the picture cards begin with the focus sound. For example, for the letter *p*, you might use a picture of a pig for the key card and pictures of a pin, a pail, a pipe, a pie, and a man for sorting. Children will then identify the pictures that have the same beginning sound as *pig* and find the one that does not fit.

5. Be sure to model the process of naming each object with the children so they are calling it by the correct name. Say aloud the name of the object on the key picture card with each word for sorting before a decision is made. You might want to isolate the first sound before saying the word, for example, "/p/, *pig*; /p/, *pin*. Yes, they both sound the same at the very beginning. *Pig, pail*. Yes, they both sound the same at the beginning." After several weeks of modeling this activity with the group, place the materials in a learning center for children to sort on their own.

6. To help the children connect sounds with letters, label the key card. Encourage children to notice that all the pictures sound the same at the

beginning and start with the same letter as the key word. Then name the letter. Figure 17 shows a child's completed picture sort for beginning sounds. Note that a card featuring a question mark may be used to indicate where a child might put the card or cards that do not fit.

7. Note that when teaching sorting, it is important to work with the whole group for short periods of time over many months before moving to a center-based activity. Notice which children are ready to sort independently and invite children to sort in a learning center when they are ready. Choose familiar sounds and sort for only one sound at a time. When a child sorts incorrectly, ask, "Why did you put this picture here?" Have the child name the picture. Gradually add more of the sounds you

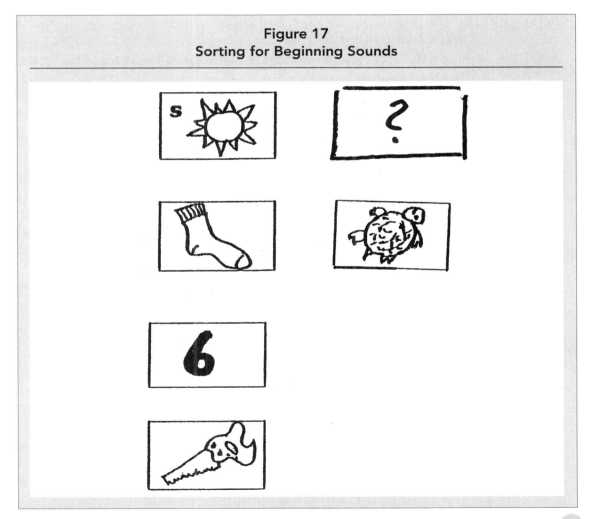

Figure 17
Sorting for Beginning Sounds

have introduced; when children are ready, add more than one word that does not fit the category.

Variation

Create a card game designed for two or three children to play in which a pile of cards with pictures on them much like the ones in Figure 17 are placed facedown on the table or desk. Children take turns taking cards from the deck. If the card has a picture that begins like the target sound, they may keep it. Otherwise it goes in a discard box or basket. When all the cards have been taken, the child with the most cards is the winner. Children can help check one another. Also, the teacher might take a quick look at the end of the game to see that the children have made correct decisions.

What to Look For

Listen for children's ability to name the pictures, listen for and isolate the beginning sounds of words, and categorize the pictures by the target sound. Have children leave their work with you when it is completed so that you can go over it with them.

How to Accommodate Differences

Accommodations for English-Language Learners. Pay special attention to any vocabulary and pronunciation differences that might interfere with the ability of English-language learners to name the pictures and sort them into the correct category. Try to anticipate which children might have problems, and give them help in advance.

Accommodations for Atypical Learners. Some children need more practice in sorting by concept than others. Categorization is a high-level cognitive operation that is used throughout the preschool curriculum. Make certain that children understand what it means to sort things into similar categories so that they are not struggling with this basic concept at the same time they are attempting to sort the beginning sounds of words. For some children, the difficulty may result from limited background knowledge of the names of the pictures to be sorted. For others, the differences between sounds may be subtle or indistinguishable at first. Try to determine what the problem might be and then ease these children into sorting by sounds through one-on-one intervention.

Accommodations for Advanced Learners. Children who are advanced learners may enjoy the challenge of sorting two sounds. You might set out two key picture cards, each representing a different initial sound. Provide cards that fit into these categories, along with some that do not. The sorting chart shown in Figure 18 features three columns of cards, one for each sound and one with a question mark for those picture cards that do not fit.

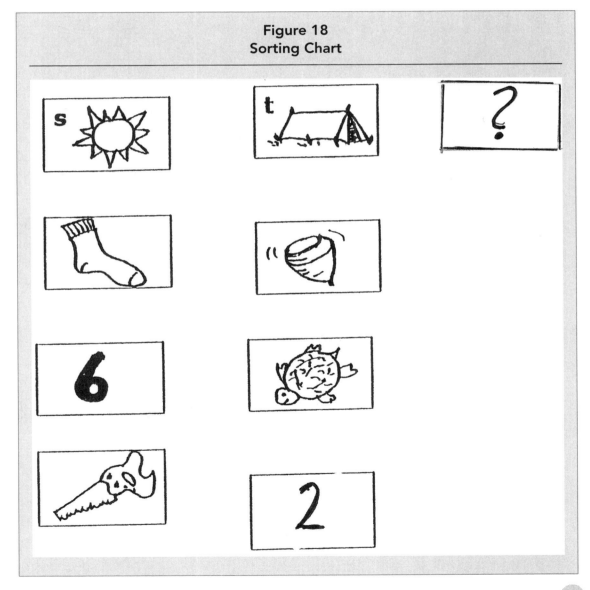

Figure 18
Sorting Chart

Figure 19
Phonemic Awareness Assessment Checklist

This checklist may be used to record observations of ongoing literacy activities. Concepts appear in order of difficulty from broad aspects of phonological awareness to phonemic awareness with a phonics connection.

The child

___ Demonstrates sensitivity to the sounds of spoken words by listening attentively and responding appropriately during phonemic awareness activities
___ Identifies rhymes and rhyming sounds in familiar words
___ Participates appropriately in rhyming games, songs, and poems by recognizing and filling in correct rhymes
___ Claps/counts the number of syllables in names and other familiar words
___ Groups picture cards or objects according to beginning sounds
___ Calls attention to words with similar beginning sounds
___ Relates some beginning sounds with the letters representing them

---

Assessing Children's Phonemic Awareness

Formal assessment of phonemic awareness is becoming increasingly common at the preschool level. Whether or not your school requires the use of a formal assessment, it is important to take advantage of daily literacy activities to monitor and document children's development of this important skill. The checklist in Figure 19 can assist you in both planning for and monitoring children's development of phonemic awareness.

Making Connections Between Home and School

Use the information in Figure 20 to create your own flier to be sent home to families or for use in a meeting with parents or other caregivers. Prepare the flier in more than one language, if necessary.

SUGGESTIONS FOR REFLECTION AND DISCUSSION, INTERACTIVE ACTIVITIES, AND FOLLOW-UP

Suggestions for Reflection and Discussion

Discuss the strategies offered in this chapter. In what ways are they similar to things you are already doing? How are they different? Discuss any changes you might make to your curriculum.

Suggestions for Interactive Activities

Observe a demonstration of a lesson that focuses on shared reading using a Big Book or chart. The demonstration may be provided by a fellow teacher or someone leading the professional development effort in your school. It may be done with children, simulated without children, or it may make use of a video that fits with the ideas offered in the chapter. Keep the chapter content in mind as you participate in a discussion of examples that illustrate understanding about language and literacy development, effective teaching, and connections to your district- or school-based standards and assessment.

Suggestions for Follow-Up

Shared reading represents a major component of the literacy program at the preschool level. Continue to reflect on and discuss its implications for learning about print. Discuss and share how you vary shared reading interaction depending on the type of text involved (e.g., narrative, informational, poetry, etc.).

Use Figure 13 as a vehicle for assessment as you work with whole or small groups and with individuals. When working with groups, you might simply make notes about what needs additional attention and follow-up. Checklists of this sort can serve as excellent tools for documentation of the progress of individuals.

CHAPTER 6

Alphabet Knowledge

As noted in Chapter 1, alphabet knowledge is an excellent predictor of success in early reading. Children who can identify some letters are demonstrating that they are noticing print, developing their visual memory, and distinguishing among letter forms. They also are able to match a letter name with its form.

This chapter presents four strategies that support children in acquiring alphabet knowledge. The first strategy, Name Games, is a broad, integrated instructional strategy designed to serve as a model for the kind of activities that teachers should use throughout the year. It addresses alphabet knowledge within a broader framework of literacy activities. The additional strategies are narrower activities that focus more specifically on alphabet knowledge. Examples of additional strategies are also given. These focused strategies concentrate on specific aspects of alphabet knowledge with connections to phonemic awareness and may be used as follow-up to whole-group instruction with small groups of children who need additional support. They may also be used for review with the whole group, if needed.

Name Games: An Integrated Instructional Strategy

What It Does

Using children's names to teach them about print is a sure way to get their attention and keep their interest. Most children learn the letters of their name before they learn any others. Children's natural desire to read, spell, and write their names offers teachers a perfect opportunity to help children explore almost all the concepts of print.

Name Games are activities that progress from easy to more difficult. Like shared writing and shared reading, this strategy is meant to be used over an extended period of time. Teachers can assess children's progress and either repeat activities or stretch children to new challenges. Name Games require only a few minutes at a time and are easily integrated into large-group time devoted to shared reading and other literacy activities.

How to Do It

1. Make a pair of identical name cards for each child in the class. Add helping pictures—photos of the children, stickers, or drawings—to the cards if you wish. Sort the cards into two sets (see Figure 21).

2. Name Match. During large-group time, give each child a name card with his or her name on it. Hold up one card at a time from your set and ask, "Whose name is this?" Have the children match their cards with the card you are holding.

   At first, the children will use the helping pictures to match. This is fine. The purpose of this game is to help them visually match items and learn the format of this large-group matching game, which will be the basis for other Name Games. After children get the idea of how the game

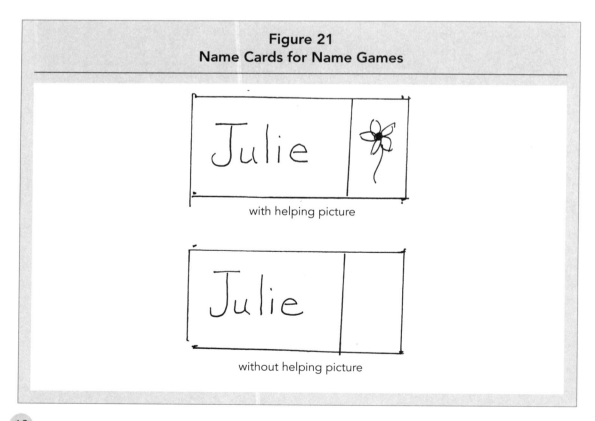

Figure 21
Name Cards for Name Games

with helping picture

without helping picture

is played, remove the part of the name card with the helping picture. Then have children match cards using only the print. Each time a child matches cards, recite the letters in his or her name. Invite the child to say the letters along with you as you point to them.

3. Who's Here? Hang a strip of Velcro at children's eye level in a convenient spot in the classroom. Attach matching Velcro strips to the backs of one set of name cards. Place the name cards in a large shallow box or on a shelf near the hanging Velcro strip.

    When children come in each morning, ask them to find their name cards and attach them to the hanging Velcro strip. During circle time, read the names together, as in Figure 22, to see who is present and who is absent. Select one or two names to read a second time, pointing to each letter as you go and encouraging children to join in. Now and then, repeat this activity in small groups or with individuals.

4. Guess the Name. Once children are somewhat familiar with their names, hold up a name card, and cover all but the first letter. Ask questions such

Figure 22
Matching Our Names

as, "Whose name could this be? It starts with the letter *J*. Charles, could this be your name? Jason, could this be your name? Who else's name could this be? Joshua? Carla?" Reveal more letters and continue in the same way. At first, do this while children are holding their copies of the name cards. Encourage them to compare the letters on their name cards to those on the card you are holding. When most of the children seem to understand the process and can identify their names, try holding on to their copies of the name cards to see if they can identify their names from memory. Ask questions about the names of the letters you are revealing.

5. Name Puzzle. Print each child's name on a business-size envelope. Make a duplicate on a piece of oaktag or stiff paper. Cut the duplicate into individual letters and place them inside the envelope. Have each child match the cut letters to the name on the outside of the envelope. Be sure to model this process during large-group time before you ask children to do this on their own. Again, name the letters when you are modeling for the children. After children have reconstructed their names with the cut-apart letters in the envelopes, assist them in spelling their names aloud (see Figure 23).

6. Letter Detectives. Display one, two, or three name cards at a time. It is best to start with one name card and work up to three once children have the idea. Show a letter card and identify the letter. Ask, "Can you find this letter in any of these names?" Many children will be able to visually match letters that are not in their names, although they may not be able to identify those letters in isolation. This is a good beginning.

For an additional challenge, ask children to find two names that have the same first letter, find two names that have the same last letter, or find the name that contains a particular letter. (This would be done without showing the letter.) Note that children need to understand the positional words *first* and *last* in order to do this activity. To assist children with this important concept, point to the beginning of the word as you say *first* and to the end of the word when you say *last*.

In the Name Games collection of activities, teachers model essential literacy behaviors, encourage children's involvement, and support the development of print concepts. The games progress from easy to difficult; each is scaffolded so that the teacher models, invites children to participate, and then encourages them to work independently as he or she monitors their progress. Here is a list of Name Game tasks in order of increasing difficulty:

Figure 23
Solving a Name Puzzle

- Recognize name with graphic support (photo or sticker)
- Recognize name without graphic support
- Apply name recognition purposefully
- Differentiate between and among names
- Reconstruct own name from individual letters
- Visually match specific letters in names
- From a set of three names, find the two names that begin or end with the same letter
- Look at a letter and find the name that has the letter at the beginning, end, or somewhere in the middle

Variations

Write Children's Names.   Find opportunities to write children's names each day. Be sure to spell aloud as you write and invite children to spell with you. Even when children write their own names, it is important to name the letters with them.

Hunt for Letters.   Have children find the letters in their names, particularly the first letter, in other places in the room, such as in alphabet books, on charts, and so on.

Letter Games.   Once children have demonstrated sufficient understanding of Name Game activities, try some of the following variations:

- Show a letter and have children name it.
- Name a letter without showing it and have children find a name with that letter.
- Ask one child to name a letter and another child to find it.
- Say a word not on the list, stressing its initial sound. Have children locate a name on the list that has the same beginning sound.

Find Names on a Helpers Chart.   Name Games can be adapted for use with a helpers chart in which children's name cards are used to indicate classroom chore assignments. Notice which children recognize their own names and those of their classmates.

What to Look For

Name Games offer an excellent opportunity to teach and assess young children's interest in and awareness of environmental print. The checklist in Figure 24 serves as a useful instrument for monitoring and documenting children's learning of concepts of print as they engage in Name Games.

How to Accommodate Differences

Accommodations for English-Language Learners.   Name Games work with names from any language because all children identify with their names. Avoid Anglicizing a child's name to make it easier for you to pronounce.

Accommodations for Atypical Learners.   Children who are developing more slowly than most might benefit from more tactile experiences. Forming their names with plastic letters or other types of three-dimensional letters can help them develop alphabet knowledge.

Figure 24
Observation Checklist for Assessing Children's Knowledge of Concepts of Print During Name Games

---

Observe children's understanding of the following concepts:

Print Conveys Meaning
___ Names have a special and powerful meaning.

Letter Order
___ The letters in a name must maintain a certain order. If the order is changed, it is no longer that name.

Concept of Word
___ A name is a word, whether spoken or written.
___ Names can be read.

Letter Knowledge
___ The letters in a name have names of their own. The letters can be found in other words as well.

Phonemic Awareness
___ Some names look and sound the same at the beginning as other names and they also look and sound like other words.

Literacy Language
___ Certain words (e.g., *word*, *letter*, letter names) help people to talk about names.

Accommodations for Advanced Learners. Children who know most of the letters of the alphabet should be encouraged to develop accuracy and fluency through bingo, lotto, and other games that make use of the alphabet. They may also sing songs such as "B-I-N-G-O" and change the first letter to *Z* or *W* to extend their alphabet knowledge. They should also be encouraged to write just for fun. However, keep in mind that some children's intellectual abilities may be far ahead of their fine-motor skills.

Focused Strategy 1: Sharing Alphabet Books

What It Does
Regular exposure to alphabet books during read-aloud time is essential to supporting children's learning of letter names.

How to Do It

1. Over time, try to add a variety of types of alphabet books to your library collection. Obtain at least two copies of each alphabet book. Use one copy for read-alouds and make the other copies accessible to the children. Alphabet books in enlarged text format (i.e., Big Books) with companion sets of little books are particularly useful. *Chicka Chicka Boom Boom* (Archambault & Martin, 1984) and *On Market Street* (Lobel, 1981) are two excellent alphabet books available in Big Book format.

> Throughout the year, introduce a new alphabet book every few weeks or so. Between new books, continue to return periodically to books already read.

2. Throughout the year, introduce a new alphabet book every few weeks or so. Between new books, continue to return periodically to books already read.

3. When using Big Books with companion sets of little books, allow two or three of the little books to be taken home for read-alouds with parents. The books can be placed in a plastic bag and be part of a take-home book circulation program.

4. Use the alphabet books in conjunction with the following activities:

   - Have children indicate letters from the books that they know in their own names and in the names of others.
   - Have children match letters from alphabet books with letters on a large wall alphabet chart placed at the children's eye level.
   - Compare alphabet books in terms of the illustrations and special features (e.g., rhyme, themes). Have children tell which ones they like best and why.

Variations

Read With a Partner.   Divide the children into pairs. Distribute a copy of a familiar alphabet book to each pair, or allow pairs to select a book of their choice. Tell them that today they are going to have fun reading together. They can take turns looking through the book page by page, or they can each hunt for letters they know and read the pages on which those letters appear. First, they should read the letter, and then they can tell about anything else they see on the page. Model the process for them, and then have two children demonstrate. Have each pair find a comfortable spot in the room to read. Use the opportunity to circulate among the children and observe evidence of their understandings about print (e.g., naming letters or handling books). Whenever possible, use a checklist to record what you notice. This activity offers children an opportunity to engage in literacy in a social way. It is especially helpful for children who rarely visit the library center on their own but enjoy working with others. Children can also try this activity alone or in groups of three.

What to Look For

Look for the children's growing ability to distinguish among letters in alphabet books of all types and to name letters accurately. Call attention to both upper- and lowercase letters. You may wish to use the terms *big* and *little* or *capital* and *small*. If possible, use terms consistent with the kindergarten program that most of the children will attend.

How to Accommodate Differences

Accommodations for English-Language Learners.   Ask a librarian about alphabet books in other languages. You may not feel comfortable reading them, and they may not be appropriate for your entire class; however, you might want to make parents and other caregivers aware of the books' availability. Keep in mind that what children learn about concepts of print in one language can be applied to a second language.

Accommodations for Atypical Learners.   All children enjoy hearing the same book over and over again. For children who are developing more slowly than most, repeated readings of the same alphabet book can be very beneficial. Encourage parents and other home caregivers to read a particular alphabet book to their children each night. Parents who have limited literacy skills often feel comfortable with this type of activity. Encourage them to let their children take the lead as often as possible.

Accommodations for Advanced Learners.   As mentioned earlier, it is important to offer children a range of alphabet books. Advanced learners will enjoy reading and browsing through the more complex alphabet books in your collection.

Focused Strategy 2: Making a Class Alphabet Book

This strategy engages children in creating a class alphabet book.

What It Does

Creation of an alphabet book helps children apply what they have learned through exposure to professionally written alphabet books. In addition to reinforcing their alphabet knowledge, children make use of virtually all they know about books and concepts of print.

How to Do It

1. Briefly show one or two of the alphabet books with which the children are familiar. Call attention to how the books are similar and how they are different. Invite the children to make their own class alphabet book.

2. Explain that the children will need to make some decisions: How many letters will appear on each page of their book? Will the letters appear in a particular order? How will the children verify that order? By checking various sources (alphabet books and charts), the children can see that there is a certain order to the alphabet.

3. Allow one page per alphabet letter. Print the letter in both uppercase and lowercase at the top of the page. Have the children illustrate each page with drawings or magazine pictures of things whose names begin with that letter. Decide whether you want to label the pictures. If so, print clearly and spell out the words as you write them.

4. This project should continue over several months. Use sturdy paper and rings to hold the pages together. Make the book accessible to the children.

5. During large-group time, periodically reread to the children the pages that have been completed. Then return the book to the library center for children to read on their own.

Variations

Personal Alphabet Books.   After completing the class alphabet book, encourage children to create their own alphabet books. Children may choose to illustrate the pages of their books or paste a cut-out magazine picture on each page. Have the children label the pages with scribbles, **letter strings**, or invented spellings. Letter strings are groups of letters written by the child with no attention to sound–letter correspondence. Often children will use whatever letters they know to represent what they want to say. For most children, this is the first step in the process toward more conventional writing. Invented spellings are often phonemically based. Although the spelling is not conventional, the child writes some letters that correspond to sounds in the word.

Individual alphabet books can be done in conjunction with the class book. Each time a letter is introduced to the class, children can follow up with a page in their personal books.

What to Look For

Look for the children's growing abilities to distinguish among letters and name them accurately. Notice their abilities to name upper- and lowercase letters.

How to Accommodate Differences

Accommodations for English-Language Learners. Occasionally label an illustration with a word from another language as well as with the English word. Show how the same letters can be used to write in both languages.

Accommodations for Atypical Learners. For children who are developing more slowly than most, recognizing letters and remembering letter names will take much more time. Concentrate on the letters in each child's name first. Gradually extend to other words important to the child—*mom*, *dad*, names of siblings, and so on.

Accommodations for Advanced Learners. Many children will know all of the upper- and lowercase letters by the age of 4. Focus children's attention on the first letter of the labeled words and to the sounds the letters represent, when applicable.

Focused Strategy 3: Using Computers to Enhance Alphabet Knowledge

This strategy requires children to use computers to extend and reinforce their alphabet knowledge.

What It Does

Computer-based activities offer children an opportunity to practice skills in engaging and varied ways. Alphabet activities to suit the level of virtually all preschool children are widely available on the Internet. Some current websites that offer alphabet activities include the following:

- Public Broadcasting System: www.pbs.org
- Reading Is Fundamental: www.rif.org
- Sesame Street: www.sesameworkshop.org
- U.S. Department of Education: www.ed.gov

How to Do It

Always preview the computer program in advance and plan for its use. Consider how you will introduce the activity, the length of time you want a child to work at a particular activity, whether the activity is more effective if children work individually or in pairs, and how you might vary its use according to student needs and abilities.

Introduce new software to the entire group, letting some children participate in the demonstration as you guide them. Move gradually to independent center-based work by first selecting children who can work alone with very little guidance. This will give others an opportunity to get a feel for what is involved in the activity. As other children are selected, give them a brief tutorial as they begin.

Variations

Take advantage of the variations built into the computer software. Adjust the software settings to match the children's abilities. Young children will need guidance in finding the level most appropriate for them. Note that in order to take advantage of software variations, it is important that you review the software carefully before introducing it to the group.

What to Look For

Ask yourself the following questions as you observe children engaged in computer-based activities:

- Is there evidence that the child is gaining a sense of control over the medium of instruction (i.e., the computer)?
- Is the child following instructions and giving mostly correct responses?
- Does the child self-correct when the wrong response is made?
- Does the child seem to be gaining confidence about his or her alphabet knowledge?

- Is there some evidence of connection between what the child is learning via the computer and what he or she is learning in other classroom activities?

How to Accommodate Differences

Accommodations for English-Language Learners.   Most computer activities are in English. Children tend to adapt easily to these materials, but English-language learners might benefit from extra help to get them started. If someone is available who speaks the children's home language, arrange for that person to give English-language learners a brief tutorial.

Accommodations for Atypical Learners.   Offer a range of computer materials to accommodate children who are developing more slowly than most. It is very important that all children gain a sense of success and accomplishment from the activities in which they engage.

Accommodations for Advanced Learners.   As with all children, the advanced learner needs to be challenged but not frustrated. These children are most likely to want new materials to explore. Some may even want to compose at the keyboard by typing their names or other words they know.

Assessing Children's Alphabet Knowledge

There are many opportunities to observe children's knowledge of letter names through the integrated activities in this chapter. We recommend that you assess the children individually at the beginning and end of the school year. You will need to allow several days for each assessment period.

For the alphabet knowledge assessment, you will need one set each of upper- and lowercase letter cards and the Letter Identification Checklist in Figure 25. Arrange the letter cards in the sequence found on the Letter Identification Checklist. Ask the child being assessed to identify the uppercase letters one at a time. (You should show one large letter at a time, not a page with multiple letters.) Continue with the lowercase letters one at a time. Place a checkmark next to the letters the child correctly identifies. Note which upper- and lowercase letters the child can identify and the number of each. To measure progress, assess children's knowledge of letter names at the beginning, middle, and end of the school year.

Figure 25
Letter Identification Checklist

Child's Name _____ Age _____ Date_____

Teacher's Name _____

Letter Names (Uppercase/ Lowercase)   **Comments** (Note incorrect name given for a letter)

A a

F f

K k

P p

W w

Z z

B b

H h

O o

J j

U u

C c

Y y

L l

Q q

M m

D d

N n

S s

X x

I i

E e

G g

R r

V v

T t

Note. Adapted from *National Head Start Summer Teacher Education Program (STEP) Teacher's Manual* (2002).

Making Connections Between Home and School

Use the information in Figure 26 to create your own flier to be sent home to parents or for use at a parents' meeting. Prepare the flier in more than one language, if necessary.

Figure 26
Information for Parents: Learning About Letters

In school we are learning about letters. We are discovering that
- The letters of the alphabet are used to make words.
- We can learn the names of all the letters.
- We can learn the letters in our name.

Learning about letters is important because

- Knowing the alphabet gives children an advantage in learning to read.
- Letter names are part of the language used to talk about reading and writing.
- Knowledge of letters is helpful in learning how letters and sounds relate to one another (phonics) and helps children to remember how words are spelled.

Here are a few ways you can help:

- Sing the alphabet song with your child.
- Read alphabet books to your child, and point to the letter on each page.
- Display your child's name in a prominent place and help him or her learn the letters.
- Provide plastic or wooden letters for your child to play with.

SUGGESTIONS FOR REFLECTION AND DISCUSSION, INTERACTIVE ACTIVITIES, AND FOLLOW-UP

Suggestions for Reflection and Discussion
Discuss the strategies offered in this chapter. How are they similar to things you are already doing? How are they different? Discuss any changes you might make to your curriculum.

Suggestions for Interactive Activities
Observe a demonstration of a lesson that focuses on alphabet knowledge. The demonstration may be provided by a fellow teacher or someone leading the professional development effort in your school. It may

be done with children, simulated without children, or it may make use of a video that fits with the ideas and strategies offered in the chapter. Keep the chapter content in mind as you participate in a discussion of examples from the demonstration that illustrate understanding about language and literacy development, effective teaching, and connections to your district- or school-based standards and assessment.

Suggestions for Follow-Up
Use Figure 27 as a vehicle for assessment as you work with whole or small groups and with individuals. When working with groups, you might simply make notes about what needs additional attention and follow-up. Checklists of this sort can serve as excellent tools for documentation of the progress of individuals.

Figure 27
Language and Literacy Checklist for Early Education and Child-Care Settings

---

1. _____ Do adults interact with children in a positive, engaging manner?
2. _____ Is the ratio of children to adults suitable for the age group, so that children can get sufficient appropriate attention?
3. _____ Do adults attempt to converse with children one-on-one and in small groups throughout the day?
4. _____ Are children read aloud to on a daily basis?
5. _____ Is the number of books available to children sufficient? A minimum of five books per child should be readily accessible to them and be rotated frequently.
6. _____ Is a variety of types of books offered for children? Does the collection include storybooks; nursery rhyme and poetry books; concept books, such as number, color, and alphabet books; and informational books about topics such as nature, trucks, and neighbors?
7. _____ Do adults model the uses of literacy, so that children begin to understand how it functions in their lives?
8. _____ Are regularly scheduled meetings held with parents in which language and literacy development are discussed?
9. _____ Are informal conversations and conferences held with parents in order to learn about the children from their parents' point of view?
10. _____ Are caregivers and educators involved in an ongoing program of professional development that supports them in fostering young children's language and literacy development?

Today, teachers of young children are expected to place a high priority on helping their students learn print concepts and practices. This book is one resource that will help teachers to do this in ways that are grounded in established knowledge about how children learn literacy as well as in what is known about developmentally appropriate practice. You can use the set of guiding principles in Figure 28 to link standards, instruction, and assessment to effectively help children learn about print.

Figure 28
Helping Young Children Learn About Print:
What Teachers Should Know

- Standards for early literacy are increasing for both children and teachers.
- Research suggests that what young children understand about print is a key predictor of later reading outcomes.
- Concepts of print include how print is used; that print carries meaning; and understandings about words, letters, and directionality.
- Alphabet knowledge is related to concepts of print.
- Phonemic awareness is an oral concept. Children who have a strong background in phonemic awareness and understand concepts of print may begin to link sounds with print.
- Learning about print should be done in a way that connects to the multiple domains of child development and the ways that young children learn best.
- A print-rich classroom environment with opportunities to use written language in meaningful ways is critical to developing children's interest in print and their understanding about how it works.
- Strategies for developing concepts of print may be broad and literature based or they may be more narrowly focused and explicit.
- Strategies should be adjusted to accommodate differences in children's abilities, linguistic backgrounds, and previous experiences with books and print.
- Informal ongoing assessment should document how well each child is progressing both individually and in terms of the class, as well as how the class is progressing as a whole. The results should be used to plan further learning experiences.

REFERENCES

Allen, K.E., & Marotz, L.R. (1994). *Developmental profiles: Birth to six*. Albany, NY: Delmar.

Almy, M., Monighan, P., Scales, B., & Van Hoorn, J. (1984). Recent research on play: The teacher's perspective. In Katz, L.G. (Ed.), *Current topics in early childhood education* (Vol. 5, pp. 1–26). Norwood, NJ: Ablex.

Anderson, R.C., Hiebert, E.H., Scott, J.A., & Wilkinson, I.A.G. (1985). *Becoming a nation of readers: The report of the Commission on Reading*. Washington, DC: National Institute of Education.

Armbruster, B.B., Lehr, F., & Osborn, J. (2003). *Put reading first: The research building blocks for teaching children to read, kindergarten through grade 3* (2nd ed.). Washington, DC: Partnership for Reading. Retrieved April 20, 2004, from www .nifl.gov/nifl/partnershipforreading/publications/PFRbooklet.pdf

Bear, D.R., Invernizzi, M., Templeton, S., & Johnston, F. (2000). *Words their way: Word study for phonics, vocabulary, and spelling instruction* (2nd ed.). Upper Saddle River, NJ: Merrill.

Bowman, B.T., Donovan, M.S., & Burns, M.S. (Eds.). (2000). *Eager to learn: Educating our preschoolers*. Washington, DC: National Academy Press.

Burns, M.S., Griffin, P., & Snow, C.E. (Eds.). (1999). *Starting out right: A guide to promoting children's reading success*. Washington, DC: National Academy Press.

Cazden, C.B. (1988). *Classroom discourse: The language of teaching and learning*. Portsmouth, NH: Heinemann.

Clay, M.M. (1979). *The early detection of reading difficulties: A diagnostic survey with recovery procedures*. Exeter, NH: Heinemann.

Diamond, M.C., & Hopson, J.L. (1999). *Magic trees of the mind: How to nurture your child's intelligence, creativity, and healthy emotions from birth through adolescence*. New York: Plume.

Dickinson, D.K., & Tabors, P.O. (2001). *Beginning literacy with language: Young children learning at home and at school*. Baltimore: Paul H. Brookes.

Duffy, G.G. (1993). Rethinking strategy instruction: Four teachers' development and their low achievers' understandings. *The Elementary School Journal, 93*(3), 231–247. doi:10.1086/461724

Halliday, M.A.K. (1969). Relevant models of language. *Educational Review, 22*(1), 26–37. doi:10.1080/0013191690220104

Hart, B., & Risley, T.R. (1995). *Meaningful differences in the everyday experience of young American children*. Baltimore: Paul H. Brookes.

Howes, C., & Marx, E. (1992). Raising questions about improving the quality of child care: Child care in the United States and France. *Early Childhood Research Quarterly, 7*(3), 347–366. doi:10.1016/0885-2006(92)90026-U

Moore, S.G. (1982). Prosocial behavior in the early years: Parent and peer influences. In B. Spodek (Ed.), *Handbook of research in early childhood education* (pp. 65–81). New York: The Free Press.

National Early Literacy Panel Report. (2009). Washington, DC: National Institute for Literacy.

National Head Start Summer Teacher Education Program (STEP) Teacher's Manual. (2002). Washington, DC: U.S. Department of Health and Human Services.

Neuman, S.B. (1999). Books make a difference: A study of access to literacy. *Reading Research Quarterly, 34*(3), 286–311. doi:10.1598/RRQ.34.3.3

Paris, S.G., Wasik, B.A., & Turner, J.C. (1991). The development of strategic readers. In R. Barr, M.L. Kamil, P.B. Mosenthal, & P.D. Pearson (Eds.), *Handbook of reading research* (Vol. 2, pp. 609–640). White Plains, NY: Longman.

Petitto, L., & Hirsh-Pasek, K., (Eds.). (2002, June). *Milestones in early language and literacy development*. Paper presented at the Conference on Children's Early Learning, Development, and School Readiness, Washington, DC.

Piaget, J. (1926). *The language and thought of the child*. London: Harcourt & Kegan Paul.

Rueda, R., & Garcia, G.E. (2002). Topic 9: How do I teach reading to English language learners? In S. Neuman, S. Stahl, N. Duke, P.D. Pearson, S. Paris, B.M. Taylor, et al., *Teaching every child to read: Frequently asked questions* (pp. 1–6). Ann Arbor, MI: Center for the Improvement of Early Reading Achievement.

Schickedanz, J. (2003). Engaging preschoolers in code learning: Some thoughts about preschool teachers' concerns. In D.M. Barone & L.M. Morrow (Eds.), *Literacy and young children: Research-based practices. Solving problems in the teaching of literacy* (pp. 121–139). New York: Guilford.

Skinner, B.F. (1974). *About behaviorism*. New York: Knopf.

Snow, C.E., Burns, M.S., & Griffin, P. (Eds.). (1998). *Preventing reading difficulties in young children*. Washington, DC: National Academy Press.

Strickland, D.S. (1998). What's basic in beginning reading? Finding common ground. *Educational Leadership, 55*(6), 6–10.

Strickland, D.S. (2004). Literacy in early childhood education: The search for balance. *Children & Families, 18*, 24–31.

Strickland, D.S., & Barnett, W.S. (2003). Literacy interventions for preschool children considered at risk: Implications for curriculum, professional development, and parent involvement. In C.M. Fairbanks, J. Worthy, B. Maloch, J.V. Hoffman, & D.L. Schallert (Eds.), *52nd yearbook of the National Reading Conference* (pp. 104–116). Oak Creek, WI: National Reading Conference.

Strickland, D.S., & Shanahan, T. (2004). Laying the groundwork for literacy: Preliminary report of the National Early Literacy Panel. *Educational Leadership, 61*, 74–77.

Tabors, P.O. (1998). What early childhood educators need to know: Developing effective programs for linguistically and culturally diverse children and families. *Young Children, 53*(6), 20–26.

Vygotsky, L.S. (1986). *Thought and language* (A. Kozulin, Trans.). Cambridge, MA: MIT Press. (Original work published 1934)

Yopp, H.K., & Yopp, R.H. (2000). *Oo-pples and Boo-noo-noos: Songs and activities for phonemic awareness* (2nd ed.). Orlando, FL: Harcourt.

CHILDREN'S LITERATURE CITED

Archambault, J., & Martin, B., Jr. (2000). *Chicka chicka boom boom.* New York: Aladdin.

Lobel, A. (1981). *On market street.* New York: Greenwillow.

Numeroff, L.J. (1985). *If you give a mouse a cookie.* New York: Harper & Row.

Sendak, M. (1979). *Higglety pigglety pop! or There must be more to life.* New York: Harper & Row.

Williams, S. (1989). *I went walking.* San Diego, CA: Harcourt.

INDEX

Note: Page numbers followed by *f* and *t* indicate figures and tables, respectively.

A

ACCOMMODATIONS: Building Words strategy for, 39–40; Clapping Our Names strategy for, 55; Making a Class Alphabet Book strategy for, 77; Matching Beginning Sounds strategy for, 57; Name Games strategy for, 72–73; Room Word Search strategy for, 38; shared reading for, 51–52; shared writing for, 34; Sharing Alphabet Books strategy for, 75; Sorting Picture Cards strategy for, 62–63; Things I Like strategy for, 36; Using Computers to Enhance Alphabet Knowledge strategy for, 79

ACTIVITIES: for awareness of shapes, forms, and symbols, 18*t*

ADULT–CHILD INTERACTION, 20–21, guidelines for, 20*f*

ADVANCED LEARNERS: Building Words strategy for, 40, 40*f*; Clapping Our Names strategy for, 55; Making a Class Alphabet Book strategy for, 77; Matching Beginning Sounds strategy for, 58, 59*f*; Name Games strategy for, 73; Room Word Search strategy for, 38; shared reading for, 52; shared writing for, 34–35; Sharing Alphabet Books strategy for, 75; Sorting Picture Cards strategy for, 63, 63*f*; Things I Like strategy for, 36; Using Computers to Enhance Alphabet Knowledge strategy for, 79

ALLEN, K.E., 6

ALMY, M., 10

ALPHABET BOOKS: making, 75–77; personal, 76–77; sharing, 73–75

ALPHABET KNOWLEDGE, 1, 4, 67–83; assessment of, 79, 80*f*; definition of, vii; and skills and strategies, 24; standards and learning experiences for, 4*t*

ANDERSON, R.C., 4

ARCHAMBAULT, J., 74

ARMBRUSTER, B.B., 3

ASSESSMENT, 23; of alphabet knowledge, 79, 80*f*; in Clapping Our Names strategy, 54–55; in Making a Class Alphabet Book strategy, 77; of Matching Beginning Sounds strategy, 57; in Name Games strategy, 72, 73*f*; of phonemic awareness, 64, 64*f*; of print awareness, 40–41, 41*f*; in Room Word Search strategy, 38; of shared reading, 50–51, 51*f*; of shared writing, 34; in Sharing Alphabet Books strategy, 75; of Sorting Picture Cards strategy, 62; in Things I Like strategy, 36; in Using Computers to Enhance Alphabet Knowledge strategy, 78–79

ATYPICAL LEARNERS: Clapping Our Names strategy for, 55; Making a Class Alphabet Book strategy for, 77; Matching Beginning Sounds strategy for, 57–58; Name Games strategy for, 72; Room Word Search strategy for, 38; shared reading strategy for, 52; shared writing strategy for, 34; Sharing Alphabet Books strategy for, 75; Sorting Picture Cards strategy for, 62; Things I Like strategy for, 36; Using Computers to Enhance Alphabet Knowledge strategy for, 79

B

BARNETT, W.S., 9

BEAR, D.R., 59

BIG BOOKS, 1, 25; alphabet, 74; for shared reading, 46, 49, 74

BLOCK PLAY AREA, 20*t*

BOOKS: assessment of handling, 41; in home, 25; making, 75–77; sharing, 73–75